MR. HORACE DINSMORE SR.

1st. WIFE

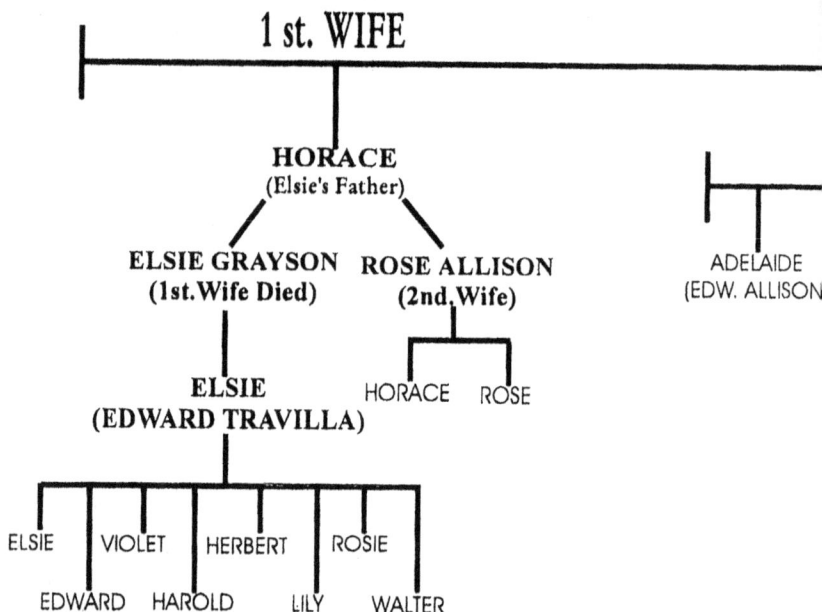

HORACE
(Elsie's Father)

ELSIE GRAYSON
(1st.Wife Died)

ROSE ALLISON
(2nd. Wife)

ADELAIDE
(EDW. ALLISON)

ELSIE
(EDWARD TRAVILLA)

HORACE   ROSE

ELSIE   VIOLET   HERBERT   ROSIE

EDWARD   HAROLD   LILY   WALTER

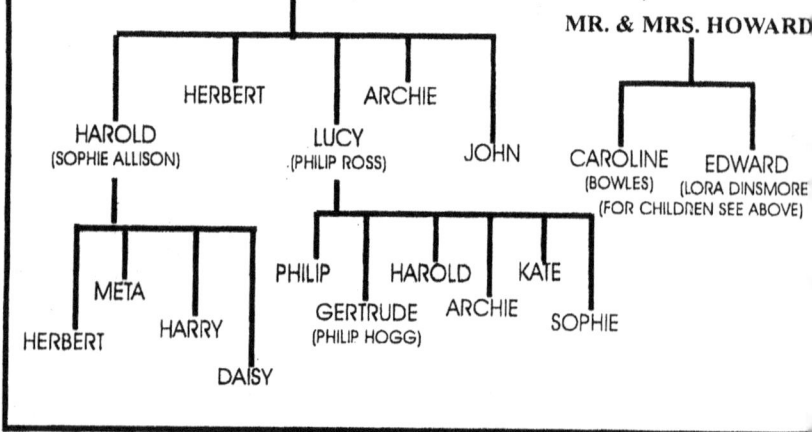

FRIENDS OF

MR. & MRS. CARRINGTON (NEPHEW-GEORGE BOYD)

MR. & MRS. HOWARD

HERBERT   ARCHIE

HAROLD
(SOPHIE ALLISON)

LUCY
(PHILIP ROSS)

JOHN

CAROLINE
(BOWLES)

EDWARD
(LORA DINSMORE)
(FOR CHILDREN SEE ABOVE)

META

HERBERT   HARRY

DAISY

PHILIP   HAROLD   KATE

GERTRUDE   ARCHIE   SOPHIE
(PHILIP HOGG)

MR. HORACE DINSMORE SR.
2 nd. WIFE

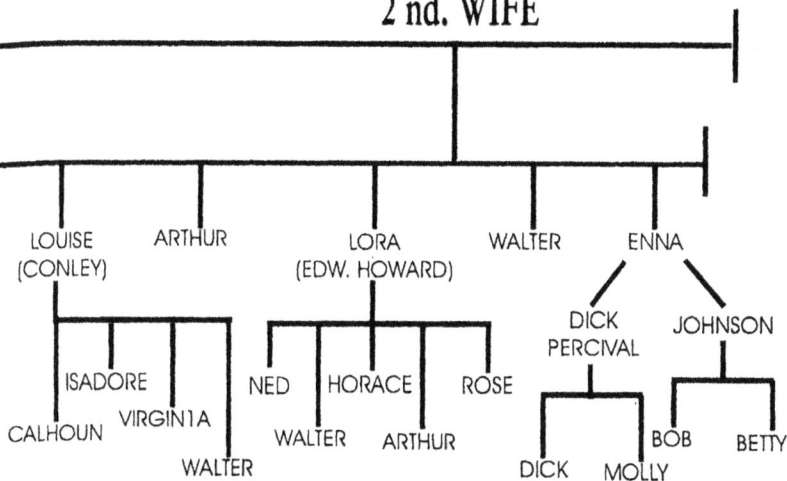

- LOUISE (CONLEY)
  - CALHOUN
  - ISADORE
  - VIRGINIA
  - WALTER
- ARTHUR
- LORA (EDW. HOWARD)
  - NED
  - WALTER
  - HORACE
  - ARTHUR
  - ROSE
- WALTER
- ENNA
  - DICK PERCIVAL
    - DICK
    - MOLLY
  - JOHNSON
    - BOB
    - BETTY

THE FAMILY
MR. & MRS. ALLISON

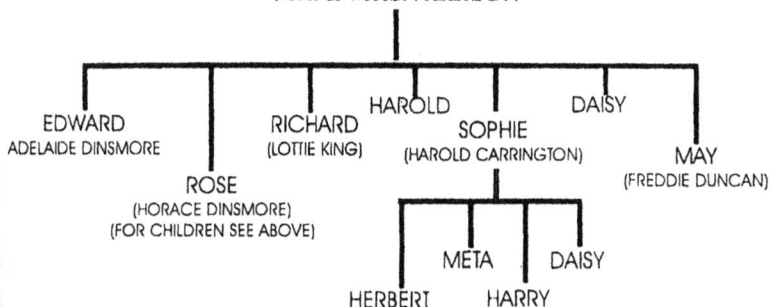

- EDWARD
  ADELAIDE DINSMORE
- ROSE
  (HORACE DINSMORE)
  (FOR CHILDREN SEE ABOVE)
- RICHARD
  (LOTTIE KING)
- HAROLD
- SOPHIE
  (HAROLD CARRINGTON)
  - HERBERT
  - META
  - HARRY
  - DAISY
- DAISY
- MAY
  (FREDDIE DUNCAN)

A LIST OF THE ELSIE BOOKS AND OTHER POPULAR BOOKS

BY

MARTHA FINLEY

Elsie Yachting With The Raymonds

A SEQUEL TO
ELSIE AND THE RAYMONDS
BOOK 15

BY
Martha Finley

Complete Authorized Edition

Published by:

Sovereign Grace Publishers, Inc.
P.O. Box 4998
Lafayette, IN 47903
Phone: (765) 429-4122
Fax: (765) 429-4142

PREFATORY NOTE.

THE Author, having received many letters from young and interested readers, has decided to acknowledge them in this way, because feeble health and much work for the publishers make it impossible to write a separate reply to each gratifying epistle.

She also desires to freely acknowledge indebtedness for much information regarding Revolutionary times and incidents, to Bancroft and Lossing; and for the routine at West Point, to an article in Harper's Magazine for July, 1887, entitled "Cadet Life at West Point," by Charles King, U. S A.

M. F.

ELSIE YACHTING WITH THE RAYMONDS.

CHAPTER I.

THE train, which for some hours had been running very fast and too noisily to admit of much conversation, suddenly slackened its speed, and Lulu turned upon her father a bright, eager look, as though some request were trembling on her tongue.

"Well, daughter, what is it?" he asked, with an indulgent smile, before she had time to utter a word.

"Oh, Papa!" she began in a quick, excited way, and quite as if she expected her request would be granted, "I know we're going through New York State, and I've just been thinking how much I would like to see Saratoga, — especially the battle-field where the Americans gained that splendid victory over the British in the Revolutionary War."

"Ah! and would Max like it, too?" the Captain asked, with a smiling glance at his son, who, sitting directly in front of them, had turned to listen to their talk just as Lulu began her reply to their father's query.

"Yes, sir; yes, indeed!" Max answered eagerly, his face growing very bright. "And you, Papa, would you enjoy it, too?"

"I think I would," said the Captain, "though it would not be for the first time; but showing the places of interest to two such ardent young patriots will more than compensate for that. — And there have been changes since I was there last," he continued, musingly. "Mount McGregor, for instance, has become a spot of historic interest. We will visit it."

"Oh, yes! where dear General Grant died," said Lulu. "I would like to go there."

"So you shall," returned her father. "This is Friday; we shall reach Saratoga Saturday night, should no accident detain us, spend Sunday there resting, according to the commandment, then Monday and Tuesday in sight-seeing."

"How nice, Papa," Lulu said with satisfaction. "I only wish Mamma Vi and Gracie could be there with us."

"It would double our pleasure," he replied. "I think we must go again some time, when we can have them along."

"Oh, I am glad to hear you say that, Papa! for I am quite sure I shall enjoy going twice to so interesting a place," said Lulu.

"I, too," said Max. "I don't know of anything that would please me better."

"I am glad to hear it, and hope there will be no disappointment to either of you," their father said.

But the train was speeding on again, too fast and too noisily for comfortable conversation, and they relapsed into silence, the Captain returning to his newspaper, Max to a book which he seemed to find very interesting, while his sister amused herself with her own thoughts.

Lulu was feeling very happy; she had been having so pleasant a summer out in the West with Papa and Maxie, and was enjoying the homeward journey, — or rather the trip to the sea-shore, where the rest of the family were, and where they all expected to remain till the end of the season, — the prospect of seeing Saratoga and its historical surroundings, and other places of interest, — a view of which could be had from the boat as they passed down the Hudson; for she and Max had both expressed a preference for that mode of travel, and their father had kindly consented to let them have their wish. She thought herself a very fortunate little girl, and wished with all her heart that Gracie could be there with them and share in all their pleasures.

Dear Gracie! they had never been separated for so long a time before, and Lulu was in such haste for the meeting now that she could almost be willing to resign the pleasure of a visit to Saratoga that they might be together the sooner. But no, oh, no, it would never do to miss a visit there! It would defer their meeting only a day or two, and she should have all the more to tell; not to Gracie only, but to Evelyn Leland and Rosie Travilla. Ah, how enjoyable that would be! Oh, how full of pleasure life was now that Papa was with them all the time, and they had such a sweet home of their very own!

With that thought she turned toward him, giving him a look of ardent affection.

He was still reading, but glanced from his paper to her just in time to catch her loving look.

"My darling!" he said, bending down to speak close to her ear, and accompanying the words with a smile full of fatherly affection. "I fear you must be growing very weary with this long journey," he added, putting an arm about her and drawing her closer to him.

"Oh, no, not so very, Papa!" she answered brightly; "but I'll be ever so glad when we get to Saratoga. Don't you think it will be quite a rest to be out of the cars for a day or two?"

"Yes; and I trust you will find them less wearisome after your three days at Saratoga."

"What time shall we reach there, Papa?" asked Max.

"Not long before your bed-time, I understand," replied the Captain.

"Then we cannot see anything before Monday?"

"You will see something of the town in walking to church day after to-morrow."

"And we can start out bright and early on Monday to visit places of interest," added Lulu; "can't we, Papa?"

"Yes, if you will be careful to be ready in good season. We want to see all we can in the two days of our stay."

"And I don't believe we'll find Lu a hindrance, as some girls would be," said Max. "She's always prompt when anything is to be done."

"I think that is quite true, Max," their father remarked, looking from one to the other with a smile that was full of paternal love and pride; "and of you as well as of your sister."

"If we are, Papa, it is because you have trained us to punctuality and promptness," returned the lad, regarding his father with eyes full of admiring filial affection.

"And because you have heeded the lessons I have given you," added the Captain. "My dear children, when I see that you are doing so, it gives me a glad and thankful heart."

They reached Saratoga the next evening more than an hour earlier than they had expected; and as the moon was nearly full, they were, much to the delight of Max and Lulu, able to wander about the town for an hour or more after tea, enjoying the sight of the beautiful grounds and residences, and the crowds of people walking and driving along the streets, or sitting in the porches. They visited Congress Park also, drank from its springs, strolled through its porches out into the grounds, wandered along the walks, and at length entered the pavilion.

Here they sat and rested for awhile; then the Captain, consulting his watch, said to his children, "It is nine o'clock, my dears; time that tired travellers were seeking their nests."

He rose as he spoke, and taking Lulu's hand, led the way, Max close in the rear.

"Yes, Papa, I'm tired enough to be very willing to go to bed," said Lulu; "but I hope we can come here again on Monday."

"I think it altogether likely we shall be able to do so," he replied.

"If we are up early enough we might run down here for a drink of the water before breakfast on Monday," said Max. "Can't we, Papa?"

"Yes, all three of us," replied the Captain. "Let us see who will be ready first."

They passed a quiet, restful Sabbath, very much as it would have been spent at home; then, on Monday morning, all three were up and dressed in season for a visit to some of the nearer springs before breakfast.

They went to the Park together, took their drinks, returned after but a few minutes spent in the garden, breakfasted, and shortly after leaving the table were in a carriage on their way to Schuylerville.

They visited the battle-ground first, then the place of surrender, with its interesting monument.

"We will look at the outside first," the Captain said, as they drew near it. "It is called the finest of its kind, and stands upon the crowning height of Burgoyne's intrenched camp."

"I wonder how high it is," Max said inquiringly, as they stood at some distance from the base, he with his head thrown back, his eyes fixed upon the top of the shaft.

"It is said to be more than four hundred and fifty feet above the level of the river," replied his father.

"Oh, I wonder if we could n't see the battle-field from the top!" exclaimed Lulu, excitedly. "I suppose they 'll let us climb up there, won't they, Papa?"

"Yes, for a consideration," returned the Captain, smiling at her eager look; "but first let us finish our survey of the outside."

"What kind of stone is this, sir?" asked Max, pointing to the base.

"Light granite," replied his father. "And the shaft is of dark granite, rough hewn, as you will notice."

"And there are gables," remarked Lulu, — "great high ones."

"Yes; nearly forty feet high, and resting at their bases upon granite eagles with folded wings. Observe, too, the polished granite columns, with carved capitals, which all the cornices of doors and windows rest upon."

"And the niches over the doors," said Max, still gazing upward as they walked slowly around the shaft, "one empty I see, each of the others with a statue in it. Oh, they are the generals who commanded our troops in the battle!"

"Yes," said his father, "Generals Schuyler, Morgan, and Gates, — who by the way was hardly worthy of the honour, as he gave evidence of cowardice, remaining two miles away from the field of battle, all ready for a possible retreat, while Burgoyne was in the thickest of the fight. The fourth and empty one, do you not see, has the name of Arnold carved underneath it."

"Oh, yes, Arnold the traitor!" exclaimed Max. "How *could* he turn against his country? But, Papa, he did do good service in this battle and some of the earlier ones, and it's such a pity he turned traitor!"

"Yes, a very great pity!" assented the Captain, heaving an involuntary sigh. "While de-

testing his treachery, I have always felt that he
has not received deserved credit for his great
services in the earlier part of the war, — the expedition to Canada, and besides smaller engagements, the terrible battle of Valcour Island,
Lake Champlain, in which he was defeated only
by the great superiority of the enemy in numbers
of both men and vessels. Though beaten, he
brought away to Ticonderoga his remaining
vessels and surviving troops. His obstinate
resistance so discouraged the British general,
Carleton, that he retired to Montreal for the
winter, which made it possible for the Northern
army to spare three thousand troops to help
Washington in striking his great blows at
Princeton and Trenton."

"And after all that, as I remember reading,"
said Max, "Congress treated Arnold shamefully, promoting other officers over his head
who neither stood so high in rank nor had done
half the service he had. I'm sure his anger at
the injustice was very natural; yet he still fought
bravely for his country, — did n't he, Papa?"

"Yes; and all that occurred some months
before this battle of Saratoga, in which he did
such service. Ah, if his career had ended there
and then, what a patriot he would now be considered! It is almost certain that if he had
been properly reinforced by Gates, he would
have inflicted a crushing defeat upon Burgoyne

at, or shortly after, the battle of Freeman's farm. But Gates was very jealous of Arnold, disliking him as a warm friend of General Schuyler, and the two had a fierce quarrel between that battle and the one of Saratoga, occasioned by Gates, prompted by his jealousy, taking some of Arnold's best troops from his command. Arnold then asked and received permission to return to Philadelphia; but the other officers, perceiving that another and decisive battle was about to be fought, persuaded Arnold to remain and share in it, as they had no confidence in Gates, who was, without doubt, a coward. He showed himself such by remaining in his tent while the battle was going on, though Burgoyne was, as I have said, in the thick of it. It was a great victory that crowned our arms on the 7th of October, 1777, and was due more to Arnold's efforts than to those of any other man, though Morgan also did a great deal to win it."

" Was n't Arnold wounded in this battle, Papa?" asked Max.

" Yes, severely, in the leg which had been hurt at Quebec. It was just at the close of the battle. He was carried on a litter to Albany, where he remained, disabled, till the next spring. One must ever detest treason and a traitor; yet I think it quite possible — even probable — that if Arnold had always received fair and just treatment, he would never have attempted to betray his country as he afterward did. Now we will go inside, and see what we can find of interest there."

The Captain led the way as he spoke.

They lingered awhile in the lower room examining with great interest the tablets and historical pictures, sculptured in bronze, *alto rilievo,* which adorned its walls.

" Oh, Papa, see ! " cried Lulu ; " here is Mrs. Schuyler setting fire to a field of wheat to keep the British from getting it, I suppose."

" Yes," her father said ; " these are Revolutionary scenes."

" Here is George III.," said Max, " consulting with his ministers how he shall subdue the Americans. Ha, ha ! they did their best, but could n't succeed. My countrymen of that day would be free."

" As Americans always will, I hope and believe," said Lulu. " I feel sure your countrywomen will anyhow."

At that her father, giving her a smile of mingled pleasure and amusement, said, " Now we will go up to the top of the shaft, and take a bird's-eye view of the surrounding country."

They climbed the winding stairway to its top, and from thence had a view of not only the battle-field, but of other historic spots also lying in all directions.

Max and Lulu were deeply interested, and

had many questions to ask, which their father answered with unfailing patience.

But, indeed, ardent patriot that he was, he keenly enjoyed making his children fully acquainted with the history of their country, and there was much connected with the surrounding scenes which it was a pleasure to relate, or remind them of, as having happened there.

From the scenes of the fight and the surrender they drove on to the Marshall place, the Captain giving the order as they reseated themselves in the carriage.

" The Marshall place, Papa? What about it? " asked Max and Lulu in a breath.

" It is a house famous for its connection with the fighting in the neighbourhood of Saratoga," replied the Captain. " It was there the Baroness Riedesel took refuge with her children on the 10th of October, 1777, about two o'clock in the afternoon, going there with her three little girls, trying to get as far from the scene of conflict as she well could."

" Oh, yes, sir ! " said Max. " I remember, now, that there was a Baron Riedesel in the British army, — a Hessian officer, in command of four thousand men ; was n't he, Papa? "

" Yes ; and his wife seems to have been a lovely woman. She nursed poor General Frazer in his dying agonies. You may remember that he was killed by one of Morgan's men in the battle of Bemis Heights, or Saratoga, fought on the 7th, — or rather, I should say, he was mortally wounded and carried to the Taylor House, where the Baroness Riedesel had prepared a dinner for the officers, which was standing partly served upon the table. He lay there in great agony until the next morning, and then died."

"Oh, yes, Papa, I remember about him!" said Lulu; "and that he was buried the same evening in the Great Redoubt, which was a part of the British intrenchments on the hills near the river."

"Yes, the strongest part," said Max. "I remember reading of it, and that the Americans opened fire on the procession from the other side of the river, not understanding what it was; so that while the chaplain was reading the service at the grave, hostile shots were ploughing up the ground at his feet, and covering the party with dust."

"Oh, Papa, won't you take us to see his grave?" asked Lulu.

"Yes, daughter, if we have time."

"Here we are, sir. This is the Marshall place," announced the driver, reining in his horses in front of a modest-looking farm-house; "and here comes a lad that'll show you round, and tell you the whole story of what happened in and about here in the time of the Revolution."

The Captain quickly alighted, helped Lulu out, and Max sprang after them.

The lad had already opened the gate, and lifted his hat with a bow and smile. "Good-morning!" he said.

Captain Raymond returned the salutation, adding, "I would like very much to show my children those parts of your house here connected with Revolutionary memories, if —"

"Oh, yes, sir; yes!" returned the boy, pleasantly. "I'll take you in and about; it's quite the thing for visitors to Saratoga to come over here on that errand."

He led the way into the house as he spoke, the Captain, Max, and Lulu following.

They passed through a hall, and on into the parlour, without meeting any one.

"This," said the lad, "is the northeast room, where Surgeon Jones was killed by a cannon-ball; perhaps you may remember about it, sir. The doctors were at work on him, cutting off a wounded leg, when a ball came in at that north-east corner and took off his other leg in its way diagonally across the room. They gave up trying to save him, then, and left him to die in yon corner," pointing to it as he spoke.

"Poor fellow!" sighed Lulu. "I can't help feeling sorry for him, though he was an enemy to my country."

"No, Miss, it was a pity, and does make one

feel sorry; for I suppose he really had no choice but to obey the orders of his king," returned the lad. "Well, the ball passed on, broke through the plank partition of the hall, and buried itself in the ground outside. They say eleven cannon-balls passed through the house in just a little while. For my part, I'd rather have been in a battle than keeping quiet here to be shot at."

"I certainly would," said the Captain.

"I, too," said Max. "I should say there was very little fun in standing such a fire with no chance to return it."

"Yes; and our people would never have fired on them if they had known they were women, children, and wounded men; but you see they — the Americans — saw people gathering here, and though the British were making the place their headquarters. So they trained their artillery on it, and opened such a fire as presently sent everybody to the cellar. Will you walk down and look at that, sir?" addressing the Captain.

"If it is convenient," he returned, following with Max and Lulu as their young guide led the way.

"Quite, sir," he answered; then, as they entered the cellar, "There have been some changes in the hundred years and more that have passed since that terrible time," he said. "You see there is but one partition wall now; there were two then, but one has been torn down, and the floor cemented. Otherwise the cellars are just as they were at the time of the fight ; only a good deal cleaner, I suspect," he added, with a smile, "for packed as they were with women, children, and wounded officers and soldiers, there must have been a good deal of filth about, as well as bad air."

"They certainly are beautifully clean, light, and sweet now, whatever they may have been on that October day of 1777," the Captain said, glancing admiringly at the rows of shining milk-pans showing a tempting display of thick yellow cream, and the great fruit-bins standing ready for the coming harvest.

"Yes, sir ; to me it seems a rather inviting-looking place at present," returned the lad, glancing from side to side with a smile of satisfaction ; "but I 've sometimes pictured it to myself as it must have looked then, — crowded, you know, with frightened women and children, and wounded officers being constantly brought in for nursing, in agonies of pain, groaning, and perhaps screaming, begging for water, which could be got only from the river, a soldier's wife bringing a small quantity at a time."

"Yes, a woman could do that, of course," said Lulu ; "for our soldiers would never fire on a woman, — certainly not for doing such a thing as that."

"No, of course not," exclaimed Max, in a

scornful tone. " American men fire on a woman
doing such a thing as that? I should say not!"

" No, indeed, I should hope not!" returned
their young conductor, leading the way from the
cellar to the upper hall, and out into the grounds.
" Yonder," he said, pointing with his finger,
" away to the southwest, Burgoyne's troops were
stationed; the German auxiliaries, too, were
resting from their fight, near Bemis Heights.
Away to the west there, Morgan's famous rifle-
men were taking up their position along Burgoyne's front and flank, while Colonel Fellows
was over yonder," turning to the east and again
pointing with his finger, " bringing his batteries
to bear upon the British. Just as the Baroness
Riedesel in her calash with her three little girls
stopped before the house, some American sharpshooters across the river levelled their muskets,
and she had barely time to push her children to
the bottom of the wagon and throw herself down
beside them, before the bullets came whistling
overhead. Neither she nor the little folks were
hurt, but a soldier belonging to their party was
badly wounded. The Baroness and her children
spent the night there in the cellar. So did other
ladies from the British army who followed her to
this retreat that afternoon. They were in one
of its three divisions, the wounded officers in
another, and the common soldiers occupied the
third."

"It must have been a dreadful night to the poor Baroness and those little girls," remarked Lulu, who was listening with keenest interest.

"Yes, indeed," responded the lad; "the cries and groans of the wounded, the darkness, dampness, and filth and stench of the wounds, all taken together, must have made an awful night for them all. I wonder, for my part, that the women and children were n't left at home in their own countries."

"That's where they ought to have been, I think," said Lulu. "Was it that night Surgeon Jones was killed?"

"No, Miss, the next day, when the Americans began firing again harder than ever."

"Where were they firing from then?" Lulu asked.

"The other side of the river, Miss; probably from some rising ground a little north of Batten Kil."

"Well, sir, what more have you to show us?" asked the Captain, pleasantly.

"A plank cut and shattered at one end, probably by the ball that killed the Surgeon. This way, if you please; here it is. And here is a rafter which you see has been partly cut in two by a shell. It was taken out of the frame of the house while they were repairing in 1868. Here are some other bits of shot and shell that have been ploughed up on the farm at different times.

Ah! there are some things at the house I should
have shown you."

"We will not mind going back so short a distance," said the Captain, "and would be glad to
see everything you have to show us."

"Yes, sir; and I think you will say these
things are worth looking at."

He led them back into the house and ex-
hibited, first, a gold coin with the figure and
inscription of George III. on one side, the British arms and an inscription with the date 1776
on the other, then a curious old musket, with
bayonet and flint lock, which was carried in the
Revolutionary War by an ancestor of the family
now residing there.

CHAPTER II.

" You may take us now to Frazer's grave,"
Captain Raymond said to the driver as they
re-entered their carriage after a cordial good-by
and liberal gift to their young guide.

" Please tell us something more about Frazer,
Papa, won't you ? " requested Lulu.

" Willingly," returned her father. " Frazer
was a brave and skilful officer ; made brigadier-
general for America only, by Carleton, in June,
1776. He helped to drive the Americans out of
Canada in that year. Burgoyne chose him to
command the light brigade which formed the
right wing of the British army, so that he was
constantly in the advance.   In the fight of October 7th he made a conspicuous figure, dressed in
the full uniform of a field-officer, mounted on a
splendid iron-gray gelding, and exerting himself
to encourage and cheer on his men. Morgan
saw how important he was to the British cause,
pointed him out to his sharpshooters, and bade
them cut him off. ' That gallant officer,' he said,
' is General Frazer. I admire and honour him ;
but it is necessary he should die, because victory

for the enemy depends upon him. Take your stations in that clump of bushes, and do your duty ! '
They obeyed, and in five minutes Frazer fell
mortally wounded, and was carried from the field
by two grenadiers. Only a few moments before
he was hit, the crupper of his horse was cut by a
rifle-ball, and directly afterward another passed
through the horse's mane, a little back of his
ears. Then his *aide* said, ' General, it is evident
that you are marked out for particular aim ;
would it not be prudent for you to retire from
this place ? ' ' My duty forbids me to retire from
danger,' Frazer answered ; and the next moment
he fell. That is Lossing's account ; and he goes
on to say that Morgan has been censured for the
order by some persons, professing to understand
the rules of war, as guilty of a highly dishonour-
able act ; also by others, who gloat over the hor-
rid details of the slaying of thousands of humble
rank-and-file men as deeds worthy of a shout for
glory, and have no tears to shed for the slaugh-
tered ones, but affect to shudder at such a cold-
blooded murder of an officer on the battle-field.
But, as Lossing justly remarks, the life of an
officer is no dearer to himself, his wife, and children, than that of a private to his, and that
the slaying of Frazer probably saved the lives
of hundreds of common soldiers."

  " Yes, Papa," returned Max, thoughtfully ;
" and so I think Morgan deserves all praise for

giving that order to his men. If Frazer did not want to lose his life, he should not have come here to help crush out liberty in this country."

"Papa, do you think he hated the Americans?" asked Lulu.

"No, I presume not; his principal motive in coming here and taking an active part in the war was probably to make a name for himself as a brave and skilful officer, — at least, so I judge from his dying exclamation, 'Oh, fatal ambition!'"

"How different he was from our Washington," exclaimed Max. "He seemed to want nothing for himself, and sought only his country's good. Papa, it does seem to me that Washington was the greatest mere man history tells of."

"I think so," responded the Captain; "he seems to have been so entirely free from selfishness, ambition, and pride. And yet he had enemies and detractors, even among those who wished well to the cause for which he was doing so much."

"Such a burning shame!" cried Lulu, her eyes flashing. "Was Gates one of them, Papa?"

"Yes; to his shame, be it said, he was. He treated Washington with much disrespect, giving him no report whatever of the victory at Saratoga. It was not until early in November that he wrote at all to the commander-in-chief, and then merely mentioned the matter incidentally.

In that month Gates was made president of the new Board of War and Ordnance, and during the following winter he joined with what is known as the 'Conway cabal' in an effort to supplant Washington in the chief command of the army."

" What a wretch ! " exclaimed Lulu. " It would have been a very bad thing for our cause if he had succeeded, — would n't it, Papa ? "

" Without doubt," answered the Captain ; " for though Gates had some very good qualities, he was far from being fit to fill the position held by Washington."

" He was n't a good Christian man, like Washington, was he, Papa ? " she asked.

" No, not by any means at that time, though it is said — I hope with truth — that he afterward became one. He was arrogant, untruthful, and had an overweening confidence in his own ability. Yet he had some noble traits ; he emancipated his slaves, and provided for those who were unable to take care of themselves. Also, he was, it is said, a good and affectionate husband and father."

" Papa, was n't it known whose shot killed Frazer ? " queried Max.

" Yes ; it was that of a rifleman named Timothy Murphy. He was posted in a small tree, took deliberate aim, and saw Frazer fall. Frazer, too, told some one he saw the man who shot him,

and that he was in a tree. Murphy was one of
Morgan's surest shots."

"I should think he must always have felt
badly about it, only that he knew he did it to
help save his country," said Lulu.

"It seemed to be necessary for the salvation
of our country," replied her father; "and no
doubt that thought prevented Murphy's conscience from troubling him."

"Did n't the Americans at first fire on the
funeral procession, Papa?" asked Lulu.

"Yes; but ceased as soon as they understood
the nature of the gathering, and at regular intervals the solemn boom of a single cannon was
heard along the valley. It was a minute-gun,
fired by the Americans in honour of their fallen
foe, the gallant dead. Ah, here we are at his
grave!" added the Captain, as horses and
vehicle came to a standstill and the carriage-
door was thrown open.

They alighted and walked about the grave and
its monument, pausing to read the inscription on
the latter.

"Though an enemy to our country, he was a
gallant man, a brave and good soldier," remarked
the Captain, reflectively.

"Yes, Papa; and I can't help feeling sorry
for him," said Lulu. "I suppose he had to obey
his king's orders of course; he could n't well
help it, and probably he had no real hatred to

the people of this country. It does seem hard
that he had to die and be buried so far away
from all he loved."

"Yes," said Max; "but he had to be killed
to save our country, since he would use his time
and talents in trying to help reduce her to slavery.
I'm sorry for him, too; but as he would put his
talents to so wrong a use, there was no choice
but to kill him, — is n't that so, Papa?"

"I think so," replied the Captain; "but it
was a great pity. Frazer was a brave officer,
idolized by his own men, and respected by even
his enemies."

"It seems sad he should lie buried so far
away from all he loved, — all his own people;
and in a strange land, too. But he could hardly
lie in a lovelier spot, I think," remarked Lulu;
"the hills, the mountains, the beautiful river,
the woods, the fields, and these tall twin pine-
trees standing like sentinels beside his grave, —
oh, I think it is just lovely! I think he showed
excellent taste in his choice of a burial-place."

"Yes, nice place enough to lie in, if one could
only be on top of the ground and able to see
what it 's like," came in hollow tones, seemingly
from the grave.

The Captain glanced at his son with a slightly
amused smile.

Lulu was startled for an instant; then, with a
little laugh, as her father took her hand and led

her back to the waiting carriage, " Oh, Maxie, that was almost too bad, though he was an enemy to our country ! " she exclaimed.

" I would n't have done it if I 'd thought it would hurt his feelings," returned Max, in a tone of mock regret ; " but I really did n't suppose he 'd know or care anything about it."

" Where now, sir ? " asked the driver as the Captain handed Lulu to her seat.

" To the Schuyler mansion," was the reply.

" Oh, I 'm glad we 're going there ! " exclaimed Lulu. " I 've always liked everything I 've heard about General Schuyler ; and I 'll be ever so glad to see the house he used to live in."

" It is n't the same house that Burgoyne caroused in the night after the battle of Bemis Heights, is it, Papa ? " asked Max.

" No ; that was burned by Burgoyne's orders a few days later," replied the Captain.

" And when was this one built ? " asked Lulu.

" That is a disputed point," said her father. " Some say it was shortly after the surrender in 1777 ; others, not until soon after the peace of 1783."

" Anyhow it was General Schuyler's house, and so we 'll be glad to see it," she said. " Papa, is it on the exact spot where the other — the first one — was ? The one Burgoyne caroused in, I mean."

"They say not, quite; that it stands a little to the west of where the first one did."

"But General Schuyler owned and lived in it, which makes it almost, if not quite, as well worth seeing as the first one would have been," said Max.

"Yes," assented the Captain. "It was on his return from Bemis Heights that Burgoyne took possession of the mansion for his headquarters; that was on the evening of the 9th of October. His troops, who had been marching through mud, water, and rain for the last twenty-four hours, with nothing to eat, encamped unfed on the wet ground near Schuylerville, while he and his cronies feasted and enjoyed themselves as though the sufferings of the common soldiery were nothing to them."

"Wasn't that the night before the day the Baroness Riedesel went to the Marshall place?" queried Max.

"Yes," replied his father. "Her husband, General Riedesel, and others, urgently remonstrated against the unnecessary and imprudent delay, and counselled hasty retreat; but Burgoyne would not listen to their prudent advice. While the storm beat upon his hungry, weary soldiers lying without on the rain-soaked ground, he and his mates held high carnival within, spending the night in merry-making, drinking, and carousing."

"What a foolish fellow!" said Max. "I wonder that he did n't rather spend it in slipping away from the Americans through the darkness and storm."

"Or in getting ready to fight them again the next day," added Lulu.

"I think there was fighting the next day, — was n't there, Papa?" said Max.

"Yes; though not a regular battle. Burgoyne was attempting a retreat, which the Americans, constantly increasing in numbers, were preventing, — destroying bridges, obstructing roads leading northward, and guarding the river to the eastward, so that the British troops could not cross it without exposure to a murderous artillery fire. At last, finding his provisions nearly exhausted, himself surrounded by more than five times his own number of troops, and all his positions commanded by his enemy's artillery, the proud British general surrendered."

"And it was a great victory, — was n't it, Papa?" asked Lulu.

"It was, indeed! and God, the God of our fathers, gave it to the American people. The time was one of the great crises of history. Before that battle things looked very dark for the people of this land; and if Burgoyne had been victorious, the probability is that the struggle for liberty would have been given up for no one knows how long. Perhaps we might have been still subject to England."

" And that would be dreadful ! " she exclaimed with warmth, — " would n't it, Max ? "

" Yes, indeed ! " he assented, his cheek flushing, and his eye kindling ; " the idea of this great country being governed by that bit of an island away across the sea ! I just feel sometimes as if I'd like to have helped with the fight."

" In that case," returned his father, with an amused look, " you would hardly be here now ; or, if you were, you would be old enough to be my grandfather."

" Then I 'm glad I was n't, sir," laughed Max ; " for I 'd rather be your son by a great deal. Papa, was n't it about that time the stars and stripes were first used ? "

" No, my son ; there was at least one used before that," the Captain said with a half smile, — " at Fort Schuyler, which was attacked by St. Leger with his band of British troops, Canadians, Indians, and Tories, early in the previous August. The garrison was without a flag when the enemy appeared before it, but soon supplied themselves by their own ingenuity, tearing shirts into strips to make the white stripes and stars, joining bits of scarlet cloth for the red stripes, and using a blue cloth cloak, belonging to one of the officers, as the groundwork for the stars.

Before sunset it was waving in the breeze over one of the bastions of the fort, and no doubt its makers gazed upon it with pride and pleasure."

"Oh, that was nice!" exclaimed Lulu. "But I don't remember about the fighting at that fort. Did St. Leger take it, Papa?"

"No; the gallant garrison held out against him till Arnold came to their relief. The story is a very interesting one; but I must reserve it for another time, as we are now nearing Schuyler's mansion."

The mansion was already in sight, and in a few moments their carriage had drawn up in front of it. They were politely received, and shown a number of interesting relics.

The first thing that attracted their attention was an artistic arrangement of arms on the wall fronting the great front door.

"Oh, what are those?" Lulu asked in eager tones, her eyes fixed upon them in an intensely interested way. "Please, sir, may I go and look at them?" addressing the gentleman who had received them and now invited them to walk in.

"Yes, certainly," he answered with a smile, and leading the way. "This," he said, touching the hilt of a sword, "was carried at the battle of Bennington by an *aide* of General Stark. This other sword, and this musket and cartridge-box, belonged to John Strover, and were carried by him in the battles of the Revolution."

"Valuable and interesting souvenirs," remarked Captain Raymond.

They were shown other relics of those troublous times, — shells, grape, knee and shoe buckles, grubbing-hooks, and other things that had been picked up on the place in the years that had elapsed since the struggle for independence. But what interested Max and Lulu still more than any of these was a beautiful teacup, from which, as the gentleman told them, General Washington, while on a visit to General Schuyler, had drunk tea made from a portion of one of those cargoes of Boston harbour fame.

"That cup must be very precious, sir," remarked Lulu, gazing admiringly at it. "If it were mine, money could n't buy it from me."

"No," he returned pleasantly; "and I am sure you would never have robbed us, as some vandal visitor did not long ago, of a saucer and plate belonging to the same set."

"No, no, indeed!" she replied with emphasis, and looking quite aghast at the very idea. "Could anybody be so wicked as that?"

"Somebody was." he said with a slight sigh;

" and it has made us feel it necessary to be more careful to whom we show such things. Now let me show you the burial-place of Thomas Lovelace," he added, leading the way out into the grounds.

" I don't remember to have heard his story, sir," said Max, as they all followed in the gentleman's wake; " but I would like to very much indeed. Papa, I suppose you know all about him."

" I presume this gentleman can tell the story far better than I," replied the Captain, with an inquiring look at their guide.

" I will do my best," he said in reply. " You know, doubtless," with a glance at Max and his sister, " what the Tories of the Revolution were. Some of them were the bitterest foes of their countrymen who were in that fearful struggle for freedom, — wicked men, who cared really for nothing but enriching themselves at the expense of others, and from covetousness became as relentless robbers and murderers of their neighbours and former friends as the very savages of the wilderness. Lovelace was one of these, and had become a terror to the inhabitants of this his native district of Saratoga. He went to Canada about the beginning of the war, and there confederated with five other men like himself to come back to this region and plunder, betray, and abduct those who were struggling for free-

dom from their British oppressors, — old neighbours, for whom he should have felt only pity and
kindness, even if he did not see things in just
the same light that they did. These miscreants
had their place of rendezvous in a large swamp,
about five miles from Colonel Van Vetchen's, cun-
ningly concealing themselves there. Robberies
in that neighbourhood became frequent, and several persons were carried off. General Stark,
then in command of the barracks north of Fish
Creek, was active and vigilant; and hearing
that Lovelace and his men had robbed General
Schuyler's house, and were planning to carry off
Colonel Van Vetchen, frustrated their design by
furnishing the Colonel with a guard. Then
Captain Dunham, who commanded a company
of militia in the neighbourhood, hearing of the
plans and doings of the marauders, at once summoned his lieutenant, ensign, orderly, and one
private to his house. They laid their plans,
waited till dark, then set out for the big swamp,
which was three miles distant. There they separated to reconnoitre, and two of them were lost;
but the other three kept together, and at dawn
came upon the hiding-place of the Tory robbers.
They were up, and just drawing on their stock-
ings. The three Americans crawled cautiously
toward them till quite near, then sprang upon a
log with a shout, levelled their muskets, and
Dunham called out, ' Surrender, or you are all

dead men!' The robbers, thinking the Americans were upon them in force, surrendered at
once, coming out one at a time without their
arms, and were marched off to General Stark's
camp, and given up to him as prisoners. They
were tried by a court-martial as spies, traitors,
and robbers; and Lovelace, who was considered
too dangerous to be allowed to escape, was
condemned to be hanged. He complained that
his sentence was unjust, and that he should
be treated as a prisoner of war; but his claim
was disallowed, and he was hanged here amid
a violent storm of wind, rain, thunder, and
lightning."

"They hung him as a spy, did they, sir?"
asked Max.

"As a spy and murderer. He was both;
and," pointing out the precise spot, "after his
execution he was buried here in a standing
posture."

"And his bones are lying right under here
are they, sir?" asked Lulu, shuddering as she
glanced down at the spot the gentleman had
indicated.

"No," was the reply; "his bones, and even
his teeth, have been carried off as relics."

"Ugh! to want such things as those for
relics!" Lulu exclaimed in a tone of emphatic
disgust.

"They are certainly not such relics as I would

care to have," returned the gentleman, with a smile. Then he told the Captain he had shown them everything he had which could be called a souvenir of the Revolutionary War, and with hearty thanks they took their leave.

CHAPTER III.

IT was dinner-time when Captain Raymond
and his children reached their hotel, and at the
conclusion of the meal they went immediately to
the station of the Mount McGregor road. There
was just time for the buying of the tickets and
seating themselves comfortably in the cars before
the train started.

"Papa, how long will it take us to go there?"
asked Lulu.

"Thirty-five minutes," he answered. "It is
about ten miles to the mountain; then we go
up about eleven hundred feet above Saratoga
Springs."

"Yes, sir," said Max; "and here on this
time-table it says that in some places the grade
is as high as two hundred and forty-six feet to
the mile."

"Set that down in your memory," returned
his father, with a smile. "Now look out of the
windows, Max and Lulu; the country is well
worth seeing."

The ride seemed very short, — it was so enjoyable, — and Lulu was quite surprised when the
car stopped and all the passengers hurried out.

Every one went into the Drexel Cottage, which was close at hand. A man showed them about, pointing out the objects of special interest, — the bed where General Grant died, the candle he had extinguished but a few minutes before breathing his last, and so on.

They spent some time in the cottage, going quietly about, looking with a sad interest at everything which had any connection with the dear departed great man, then went on up to the mountain top, where stood a large hotel. They passed it, and went on to the edge of the mountain, which overlooks the Hudson River valley.

"Oh, what a lovely view!" cried Lulu, in delight. "What mountains are those, Papa?"

"Those to the east," he replied, pointing in that direction as he spoke, "are the Green Mountains, those to the north are the Adirondacks, and those to the south the Catskills."

"Oh, Lu, look yonder!" cried Max. "There's Schuylerville with its monument, I do believe, — is n't it, Papa?"

"Yes, you are right, — the place of Burgoyne's surrender, which we visited this morning," the Captain answered. "Now suppose we go to the observatory at the top of the hotel, and take the view from there."

Max and Lulu gave an eager assent to the proposal. There were a good many stairs to climb, but the view fully repaid them for the exertion. They spent some minutes in gazing upon it, then descended and wandered through the woods till the train was ready to start down the mountain.

Max and Lulu were tired enough to go to bed at dark; and the next morning they took an early train to Albany, where they boarded a fine steamer, which would carry them down the Hudson River to West Point, where, to the children's great delight, their father had promised to stay a day or two, and show them all of historical interest connected with the spot.

It was the first trip on the Hudson that Max or his sister had ever taken, and they enjoyed it greatly, — all the more because their father was sufficiently familiar with the scenes through which they were passing to call their attention to whatever was best worth noticing, and give all desired information in regard to it, doing so in the kindest and pleasantest manner possible. The weather was all that could be desired, — cloudy, with an occasional shower, seldom heavy enough to obscure the view to any great extent, and just cooling the air pleasantly, as Lulu remarked with much satisfaction.

It was not raining when they landed at West Point, though clouds still veiled the sun. They took a carriage near the wharf, and drove to the hotel. As they alighted, some gentlemen were talking upon its porch, one of whom was in military uniform.

"Raymond, this is a meeting as delightful as unexpected, — to me at least!" he exclaimed, coming hastily forward with outstretched hand.

"Keith, I don't know when I have had a pleasanter surprise!" returned Captain Raymond, taking the offered hand and shaking it heartily, while his eyes shone with pleasure. "You are not here permanently?"

"No; only on a furlough. And you?"

"Just for a day or two, to show my children our military academy and the points of historical interest in its vicinity," replied Captain Raymond, glancing down upon them with a smile of fatherly pride and affection. "Max and Lulu, this gentleman is Lieutenant Keith, of whom you have sometimes heard me speak, and whom your mamma calls Cousin Donald."

"Your children, are they? Ah, I think I might have known them anywhere from their remarkable resemblance to you, Raymond!" Mr. Keith said, shaking hands first with Lulu, then with Max.

He chatted pleasantly with them for a few minutes, while their father attended to engaging rooms and having the baggage taken up to them. When he rejoined them Keith asked,

" May I have the pleasure of showing you about, Raymond? "

" Thank you; no better escort could be desired," replied the Captain, heartily, " you being a valued friend just met after a long separation, and also an old resident here, thoroughly competent for the task, and thoroughly acquainted with all the points of interest."

" I think I may say I am that," returned Keith, with a smile; " and it will give me the greatest pleasure to show them to you, — as great, doubtless, as you seemed to find some years ago in showing me over your man-of-war. But first, let us take a view from the porch here. Yonder," pointing in a westerly direction, " at the foot of the hills, are the dwellings of the officers and professors. In front of them you see the parade-ground; there, on the south side, are the barracks. There is the Grecian chapel, yonder the library building, with its domed turrets, and there are the mess hall and hospital." Then turning toward the west again, " That lofty summit," he said, " is Mount Independence, and the ruins that crown it are those of 'Old Fort Put.' That still loftier peak is Redoubt Hill. There, a little to the north, you see Old Cro' Nest and Butter Hill. Now, directly north, through that magnificent cleft in the hills, you can see Newburgh and its bay. Of the scenery in the east we

will have a better view from the ruins of
' Old Put.' "

" No doubt," said the Captain. " Shall we go
up there at once? "

" If you like, Raymond. I always enjoy the
view; it more than pays for the climb. But,"
and Mr. Keith glanced somewhat doubtfully at
Lulu, " shall we not take a carriage? I fear the
walk may be too much for your little girl."

" What do you say, Lulu? " her father asked
with a smiling glance at her.

" Oh, I 'd rather walk, Papa! " she exclaimed.
" We have been riding so much for the last week
and more; and you know I 'm strong and well,
and dearly love to climb rocks and hills."

" Very well, you shall do as you like, and
have the help of Papa's hand over the hard
places," he said, offering it as he spoke.

She put hers into it with a glad look and smile
up into his face that almost made Donald Keith
envy the Captain the joys of fatherhood.

They set off at once. Lulu found it a rather
hard climb, or that it would have been without
her father's helping hand; but the top of Mount
Independence was at length reached, and the little party stood among the ruins of Fort Putnam.
They stood on its ramparts recovering breath
after the ascent, their faces turned toward the
east, silently gazing upon the beautiful panorama
spread out at their feet.

It was the Captain who broke the silence. " You see that range of hills on the farther side of the river, children?"

" Yes, sir," both replied with an inquiring look up into his face.

" In the time of the Revolution every pinnacle was fortified, and on each a watch-fire burned," he said.

" They had a battery on each, Papa?" queried Max.

" Yes; but yonder, at their foot, stands something that will interest you still more, — the Beverly House, from which Arnold the traitor fled to the British ship 'Vulture,' on learning that André had been taken."

" Oh, is it, sir?" exclaimed Max, in a tone of intense interest. " How I would like to visit it, — can we, Papa?"

" I, too; oh, very much!" said Lulu. " Please take us there, — won't you, Papa?"

" I fear there will be hardly time, my dears; but I will see about it," was the indulgent reply.

" You have been here before, Raymond?" Mr. Keith said inquiringly.

" Yes; on my first bridal trip," the Captain answered in a low, moved tone, and sighing slightly as the words left his lips.

" With our own mother, Papa?" asked Lulu, softly, looking up into his face with eyes full of love and sympathy.

"Yes, daughter; and she enjoyed the view very much as you are doing now."

"I'm glad; I like to think she saw it once."

An affectionate pressure of the hand he held was his only reply. Then turning to his friend, "It is a grand view, Keith," he said; "and one that always stirs the patriotism in my blood, inherited from ancestors who battled for freedom in those Revolutionary days."

"It is just so with myself," replied Keith; "and the view is a grand one in itself, though there were no such association, — a superb panorama! The beautiful, majestic river sweeping about the rock-bound promontory below us there, with its tented field; yonder the distant spires of Newburgh, and the bright waters of its bay, seen through that magnificent cleft in the hills," pointing with his finger as he spoke, — "ah, how often I have seen it all in imagination when out in the far West scouting over arid plains, and among desolate barren hills and mountains, where savages and wild beasts abound! At times an irrepressible longing for this very view has come over me, — a sort of homesickness, most difficult to shake off."

"Such as years in the ports of foreign lands have sometimes brought upon me," observed the Captain, giving his friend a look of heartfelt sympathy.

"Dear Papa, I'm so glad that is all over,"

Lulu said softly, leaning lovingly up against him as she spoke, and again lifting to his eyes her own so full of sympathy and affection. "Oh, it is so pleasant to have you always at home with us!"

A smile and an affectionate pressure of the little soft white hand he held were his only reply.

"Ah, my little girl, when Papa sees a man-of-war again, he will be likely to wish himself back in the service once more!" remarked Keith, in a sportive tone, regarding her with laughing eyes.

"No, sir, I don't believe it," she returned stoutly. "Papa loves his home and wife and children too well for that; besides, he has resigned from the navy, and I don't believe they'd take him back again."

"Well, Lu," said Max, "that's a pretty way to talk about Papa! Now, it's my firm conviction that they'd be only too glad to get him back."

"That's right, Max; stand up for your father always," laughed Keith. "He is worthy of it; and I don't doubt the government would be ready to accept his services should he offer them."

"Of course," laughed the Captain; "but I intend to give them those of my son instead," turning a look upon Max so proudly tender and appreciative that the lad's young heart bounded with joy.

"Ah, is that so?" said Keith, gazing appreciatively into the lad's bright young face. "Well, I have no doubt he will do you credit. Max, my boy, never forget that you have the credit of an honourable name to sustain, and that in so doing you will make your father a proud and happy man."

"That is what I want to do, sir," replied Max, modestly. Then hastily changing the subject, "Papa, is that town over there Phillipstown?"

"Yes; what do you remember about it?"

"That a part of our Revolutionary army was camped there in 1781. And there, over to the left, is Constitution Island, — is n't it, sir?"

"Yes," answered his father; then went on to tell of the building of the fort from which the island takes its name, and its abandonment a few days after the capture by the British of Forts Clinton and Montgomery, near the lower entrance to the Highlands, in 1777.

"Such a pity, after they had been to all the expense and trouble of building it!" remarked Lulu.

"Yes, quite a waste," said Max; "but war's a wasteful business anyway it can be managed."

"Quite true, Max," said Mr. Keith; "and soldier though I am, I sincerely hope we may have no more of it in this land."

"No, sir; but the best way to keep out of it

is to show ourselves ready for self-defence. That
is what Papa says."

" And I entirely agree with him. Shall we go
now, Raymond, and see what of interest is to be
found in the buildings and about the grounds of
the academy? "

The Captain gave a ready assent, and they
retraced their steps, he helping Lulu down the
mountain as he had helped her up.

Keith took them, first, to the artillery labo-
ratory to see, as he said, some trophies and relics
of the Revolution. Conducting them to the centre
of the court, " Here," he remarked, " are some
interesting ones," pointing, as he spoke, to several cannon lying in a heap, and encircled by some
links of an enormous chain.

" Oh," exclaimed Max, " is that part of the
great chain that was stretched across the Hudson, down there by Constitution Island, in the
time of the Revolution? "

" Yes," replied Keith. " And these two brass
mortars were taken from Burgoyne at Saratoga ;
this larger one, Wayne took from the British at
Stony Point. I dare say you and your sister are
acquainted with the story of that famous exploit."

" Oh, yes, sir ! " they both replied ; and Lulu
asked, " Is that the English coat-of-arms on the
big cannon? "

Her look directed the query to her father, and
he answered, " Yes."

"And what do these words below it mean, Papa, — ' Aschaleh fecit, 1741 ' ? "

" Aschaleh is doubtless the name of the maker ; *'fecit'* means he executed it, and 1741 gives the time when it was done."

" Thank you, sir," she said. " Is there any story about that one ? " pointing to another cannon quite near at hand.

" Yes," he said ; " by its premature discharge, in 1817, a cadet named Lowe was killed. In the cemetery is a beautiful monument to his memory."

" Here are two brass field-pieces, each marked ' G. R.,' " said Max. " Do those letters stand for George Rex, — King George, — Papa ? "

" Yes ; that was the monogram of the king."

" And the cannon is fourteen years younger than those others," remarked Lulu ; " for, see there, it says, ' W. Bowen fecit, 1755.' "

" Oh, here's an inscription ! " exclaimed Max, and read aloud, " ' Taken from the British army, and presented, by order of the United States, in Congress assembled, to Major-General Green, as a monument of their high sense of the wisdom, fortitude, and military talents which distinguished his command in the Southern department, and of the eminent services which, amid complicated dangers and difficulties, he performed for his country. October 18th, 1783.'

Oh, that was right!" supplemented the lad, "for I do think Green was a splendid fellow."

"He was, indeed!" said the Captain; "and he has at last been given such a monument as he should have had very many years sooner."

"Where is it, Papa?" asked Lulu.

"In Washington. It is an equestrian statue, by Henry Kirke Brown."

"Yes; and very glad I am that even that tardy act of justice has been done him, — one of the bravest and most skilful commanders of our Revolutionary War," remarked Mr. Keith. Then he added, "I think we have seen about all you will care for here, Raymond, and that you might enjoy going out upon the parade-ground now. The sun is near setting, and the battalion will form presently, and go through some interesting exercises."

"Thank you!" the Captain said. "Let us, then, go at once, for I see Max and his sister are eager for the treat," he added, with a smiling glance from one brightly expectant young face the other.

CHAPTER IV.

THEY reached the parade-ground just in time to see the battalion forming under arms, and Max and Lulu watched every movement with intense interest and delight, — the long skirmish lines firing in advance or retreat, picking off distant imaginary leaders of a pretended enemy in reply to the ringing skirmish calls of the key-bugles, deploying at the run, rallying at the reserves and around the colours.

That last seemed to delight Lulu more than anything else. " Oh," she exclaimed, " is n't it lovely ! Would n't they all fight for the dear old flag if an enemy should come and try to tear it down ! "

" I 'm inclined to think they would," returned Mr. Keith, smiling at her enthusiasm. " Now look at the flag waving from the top of the staff yonder."

The words had scarcely left his lips when there came the sudden bang of the sunset gun, and the flag quickly fluttered to the earth.

Then followed the march of the cadets to their supper, and our little party turned about and went in search of theirs.

On leaving the table they went out upon the
hotel porch and seated themselves where the
view was particularly fine, the gentlemen conversing, Max and Lulu listening, both tired
enough to be quite willing to sit still.

The talk, which was principally of ordnance
and various matters connected with army and
navy, had greater interest for the boy than for
his sister, and Lulu soon laid her head on her
father's shoulder, and was presently in the land
of dreams.

"My poor, tired, little girl!" he said, low and
tenderly, softly smoothing the hair from her fore-
head as he spoke.

At that she roused, and lifting her head, said
coaxingly, "Please don't send me to bed yet,
Papa! I'm wide awake now."

"Are you, indeed?" he laughed. "I think
those eyes look rather heavy; but you may sit
up now if you will agree to sleep in the morning
when Max and I will probably be going out to
see the cadets begin their day. Would you like
to go, Max?"

"Yes, indeed, sir!" answered Max, in eager
tones; "it's about five o'clock we have to start,
— is n't it?"

"Yes, Max. Lieutenant Keith has kindly
offered to call us in season, and become our
escort to the camp."

"Oh, Papa, may n't I go too?" pleaded Lulu,

in the most coaxing tones. "I won't give you
the least bit of trouble."

"You never do, daughter, in regard to such
matters; you are always prompt, and ready in
good season."

"Then do you say I may go, Papa?"

"Yes, if you will go to bed at once, in order
to secure enough sleep by five o'clock in the
morning."

"Oh, thank you, sir! Yes, indeed, I will,"
she said, hastily rising to her feet, and bidding
good-night to Mr. Keith."

"I, too," said Max, following her example.

"Good children," said their father; then noticing the longing look in Lulu's eyes, he excused
himself to his friend, saying he would join him
again presently, and went with them.

"That is a beautiful, bright, engaging, little
girl of yours, Raymond, — one that any father
might be proud of," remarked Keith when the
Captain had resumed the seat by his side.

"She seems all that to me; but I have sometimes thought it might be the blindness of pa-
rental affection that makes the child so lovely
and engaging in her father's eyes," returned the
Captain, in tones that spoke much gratification.

"I think, indeed I am sure, not," returned
Keith. "About how old is she?"

"Thirteen. Actually, she'll be a woman before I know it!" was the added exclamation in

a tone of dismay. "I don't like the thought of losing my little girl even in that way."

"Ah, you'll be likely to lose her in another before many years!" laughed his friend. "She'll make a lovely woman, Raymond!"

"I think you are right," answered the father; "and I confess that the thought of another gaining the first place in her heart — which I know is mine now — is far from pleasant to me. Well, it cannot be for some years yet, and I shall try not to think of it. Perhaps she may never care to leave her father."

"I don't believe she will if she is wise. You are a fortunate man, Raymond! Your son — the image of his father — is not less attractive than his sister, and evidently a remarkably intelligent lad. He will make his mark in the navy; and I dare say we shall have the pleasure of seeing him an admiral by the time we — you and I — are gray-headed, old veterans."

"Perhaps so," returned the Captain, with a pleased smile; "but promotion is slow in the navy in these days of peace."

"Quite true; and as true of the army as of the navy. But even that is to be preferred to war, — eh, Raymond?"

"Most decidedly," was the emphatic reply.

"You leave for home to-morrow evening, I think you said?" was Keith's next remark, made in an inquiring tone.

"That is my plan at present," replied the Captain, "though I would stay a little longer rather than have the children disappointed in their hope of seeing everything about here that has any connection with the Revolution."

"They seem to be ardent young patriots," said Keith. "It does one good to see their pride and delight in the flag. How their eyes shone at the sight of the rally round the colours."

"Yes; and they feel an intense interest in everything that has any connection with the Revolutionary struggle. They get it in the blood; and it has been their father's earnest endeavour to cultivate in them an ardent love of country."

"In which he has evidently been remarkably successful," returned Keith. "I am much mistaken if that boy does not do you great credit while in the Naval Academy, and, as I remarked a moment since, after fairly entering the service."

"A kind and pleasant prediction, Keith," the Captain said, giving his friend a gratified look.

"How many children have you, Raymond?" was the next question.

"Only five," the Captain said, with a happy laugh, — "five treasures that should, it seems to me, make any man feel rich; also, a sweet, beautiful, young wife, who is to her husband worth far more than her weight in gold. 'Her

price is above rubies.' And you, Keith, — you
have not told me whether you have yet found
your mate."

" No, not yet. I sometimes think I never shall,
but shall soon become a confirmed old bachelor,"
Keith replied. Then, after an instant's pause,
"I wonder if Lulu's father would give her to me
should I wait patiently till she is old enough to
know her own mind in such matters, and then
succeed in winning her heart?"

" Ah, Keith, is that a serious thought or a
mere idle jest?" queried the Captain, turning a
surprised and not altogether pleased look upon
his friend.

" A sort of mixture of the two, I believe, Raymond," was the laughing reply; " but I have n't
the least idea of putting any such mischief into
your daughter's head, — at least, not at present.
But if I ask your permission half a dozen years
hence to pay my court to her, I hope it will not
be refused."

" Well, Keith," the Captain said, after a moment's silence, " I should be very loath to stand
in the way of your happiness, — still more of
that of my dear daughter; but the time is so far
off that we need not discuss the question now.
My little girl seems still the merest child, with
no thought of the cares, pleasures, and duties of
womanhood ; and I wish to keep her so as long
as I can. That is one reason why I rejoice in

being able to educate her myself in our own home; and thus far the loves of the dear ones in it have seemed all-sufficient for her happiness. And I own to being particularly pleased with her oft-repeated assurance that she loves Papa better than she does any one else in all the wide world."

"Ah, I do not wonder that she does, for her father is altogether worthy of all the love she can give him!" Keith said, with a half-sigh, thinking of the loneliness of his lot compared with that of the Captain.

"Keith," the Captain said, after a moment's silence, "you tell me your furlough will not expire for some weeks yet. Can you not spend them with us at the sea-shore?"

Donald demurred a little at first, saying he had made other plans; and besides, his going might interfere with his cousins' arrangements.

"Not the slightest danger of that," the Captain averred; "and I am certain that one and all will be delighted to see you."

"And I own to being fairly hungry for a sight of them," laughed Donald. "So, Raymond, your invitation is accepted, and on your own head be the consequences."

"No objection to that; I'm delighted to have you on any terms, reasonable or otherwise," the Captain said, with his pleasant smile.

Max and Lulu had an hour or more of

good refreshing sleep before the two gentlemen separated for the night.

Captain Raymond went very softly into Lulu's room, and stood for a moment by the bedside looking fondly down into the rosy, sleeping face, then, bending over her, kissed her tenderly on cheek and lip and brow.

Her eyes opened wide and looked up into his, while a glad smile broke over her face.

"You dear, good Papa, to come in and kiss me again!" she said, putting her arm round his neck and returning his caresses. "Oh, I do think I have just the very dearest, kindest, best father in the whole wide world!"

"That's rather strong, is n't it?" he returned, laughing, but at the same time gathering her up in his arms for a moment's petting and fondling. Then, laying her down again, "I did not mean to wake you," he said; "and I want you now to go to sleep again as fast as you can, because, though to-morrow will, I hope, be a very enjoyable day to you and Max, it is probable you will find it quite fatiguing also."

"Yes, sir; but I don't mean to think about it now, else I'd be wide awake presently, and maybe not sleep any more to-night," Lulu answered drowsily, her eyes closing while she spoke.

He was turning away, when she roused sufficiently to ask another question. "Papa, will you please wake me when the time comes to get up?"

"Yes, daughter," he replied. "Do not let the fear of not waking in season rob you of a moment's sleep. I think you may safely trust to your father to attend to that for you."

It seemed to Lulu that but a few moments had passed when her father's voice spoke again close to her side.

"Wake up now, little daughter, if you want to go with Papa and Max to see what the cadets will be doing in their camp for the next hour or so."

"Oh, yes, indeed, I do!" she cried, wide awake in an instant. "Good-morning; and thank you ever so much for calling me, dear Papa!" and with the words her arms were round his neck, her kisses on his cheek.

He gave her a hearty embrace in turn; and then, with a "Now, my darling, you must make haste, we have only ten minutes; but I shall bring you back to rearrange your toilet before going down to breakfast," he released her and went back to his own room.

Lulu made quick work of her dressing, and when her father tapped at her door to say it was time to go, was quite ready.

They found Mr. Keith waiting on the porch, exchanged a pleasant "good-morning" with him, and at once started for the camp.

Max and Lulu were in gayest spirits, and were allowed to laugh and talk till the little party drew near the camp, when their father bade them be quiet, and amuse themselves for the present by looking and listening.

He spoke in a kind, pleasant tone, and they obeyed at once.

Down by the guard-tents they could see a dim, drowsy gleam, as of a lantern; the gas-jets along the way seemed to burn dimly, too, as the daylight grew stronger, and up about the hill-tops on the farther side of the river the sky was growing rosy and bright with the coming day. But all was so quiet, so still, where the tents were that it seemed as if everybody there must be still wrapped in slumber; and Lulu was beginning to think Mr. Keith must have called for them a little earlier than necessary, when a sudden gleam and rattle among the trees almost made her jump, so startled was she, while at the same instant a stern, boyish voice called out, "Who comes there?" and a sentry stood before them wrapped in an overcoat, — for the morning was very cool up there among the mountains, — and with the dew dripping from his cap.

"Friends, with the countersign," replied Mr. Keith.

"Halt, friends! Advance one with the countersign," commanded the sentry; and while the Captain and his children stood still where they

were, Mr. Keith stepped up to the levelled bayonet and whispered a word or two in the ear of
the young sentinel which at once caused a change
in his attitude toward our party, — respectful attention taking the place of the fierce suspicion.
"Advance, friends!" he said, bringing his heels
together and his rifle to the carry, then stood like
a statue while they passed on into the camp he
guarded.

Max and Lulu, remembering their father's
order to them to keep quiet, said nothing, but
were careful to make the very best use of their
eyes.

Down by the tents, on the south and east sides,
they could see sentries pacing their rounds, but
there was as yet no sound or movement among
the occupants.

Some drummer-boys were hurrying over the
plain toward the camp, while a corporal and two
cadets were silently crossing to the northeast
corner, where stood a field-piece dripping with
dew.

Max motioned to Lulu to notice what they
were doing, and as he did so they had reached
the gun, and there was a dull thud as they
rammed home their cartridge.

The drummer-boys were chattering together in
low tones, glancing now and again at the clock
in the "Academic" tower over on the other side
of the plain. Suddenly a mellow stroke began

to tell the hour, but the next was drowned in the roar of the gun as it belched forth fire and smoke, while at the same instant drum and fife broke forth in the stirring strains of the reveille.

Lulu almost danced with delight, looking up into her father's face with eyes shining with pleasure. His answering smile was both fond and indulgent as he took the small white hand in his with a loving clasp; but it was no time for words amid the thunder of the drums playing their march in and about the camp.

Lulu could see the tent-flaps raised, drowsy heads peering out, then dozens of erect, slender lads, in white trousers and tight-fitting coatees, coming out with buckets, and hurrying away to the water-tanks and back again.

Presently the drums and fifes ceased their music; there was a brief interval of silence, while the streets of the camp filled up with gray and white coated figures. Then came another rattle of the drums like a sharp, quick, imperative call.

"Fall in!" ordered the sergeants; and like a flash each company sprang into two long columns.

"Left face!" ordered each first sergeant, while the second sergeant, answering to his own name, was watching with eagle eye a delinquent who came hurrying on, and took his place in the ranks too late by a full half-second.

"Ah," exclaimed Keith, "that poor lad will be reported as too late at reveille!"

Lulu gave him a look of surprise. "Dear me," she said to herself, "if Papa was that strict with his children what ever would become of me?"

But the first sergeant was calling the roll, and she listened with fresh astonishment as he rattled off the seventy or eighty names without so much as an instant's pause, using no list, and seeming to recognize each lad as he answered "Here."

It took scarcely a minute; then at a single word the ranks scattered, the lads hurrying away to their tents, while the first sergeant made a brief report to the captain, who stood near, then the captain to the officer of the day.

Our little party had now seated themselves where a good view of the camp might be obtained, and Max and Lulu watched with great interest what was going on there. They could see the lads pull off their gray coats, raise their tent-walls to give free circulation through them to the sweet morning air, pile up their bedding, and sweep their floors.

Lulu gave her father an inquiring look, and he said, "What is it, daughter? You may talk now, if you wish."

"I was just wondering if you had to do such work as that at Annapolis" she said in reply.

"I did," he responded, with a smile, "and thought you had heard me speak of it."

"Maybe I have," she said, with a tone and look as if trying to recall something in the past. "Oh, yes, I do remember it now! And I suppose that's the reason you have always been so particular with us about keeping our rooms nice and neat."

"Partly, I believe," he returned, softly patting the hand she had laid on his knee; "but my mother was very neat and orderly, and from my earliest childhood tried to teach me to be the same."

"And I think I'll find it easier because of your teachings, sir," remarked Max.

"I hope so," the Captain said; "you'll find you have enough to learn, my boy, without that."

"A good father is a great blessing, Max, as I have found in my own experience," said Mr. Keith.

But the roll of the drums began again, now playing "Pease upon a Trencher;" again the ranks were formed, rolls called; the sergeants marched their companies to the colour line, officers took their stations; first captain ordered attention, swung the battalion into column of platoons to the left, ordered "Forward, guide right, march!" and away they went, to the stirring music of the fifes and drums, away across the plain till the main road was reached, down the shaded lane between the old "Academic" and the chapel, past the new quarters, and the grassy terrace beyond. Then each platoon wheeled in succession to the right, mounted the broad stone steps, and disappeared beneath the portals of the mess hall.

Our party, who had followed at so slight a distance as to be able to keep the cadets in sight to the door of entrance, did not attempt to look in upon them at their meal, but hurried on to the hotel to give attention to their own breakfasts, — the keen morning air and the exercise of walking having bestowed upon each one an excellent appetite.

Max and Lulu were very eager to "get back in time to see everything," as they expressed it, so began eating in great haste.

Their father gently admonished them to be more deliberate.

"You must not forget," he said, "that food must be thoroughly masticated in order to digest properly; and those who indulge in eating at such a rapid rate will be very likely soon to suffer from indigestion."

"And we may as well take our time," added Mr. Keith, "for it will be an hour or more before anything of special interest will be going on among the cadets."

"What do they do next, sir?" asked Max.

"Morning drill, which is not very interesting, comes next; then the tents are put in order."

"That must take a good while," remarked Lulu.

"From three to five minutes, perhaps."

"Oh!" she cried in surprise; "how can they do it so quickly? I'm sure I could n't put my room at home in good order in less than ten minutes."

"But, then, you're not a boy, you know," laughed Max.

"I'm quite as smart as if I were," she returned promptly. "Is n't that so, Papa?"

"I have known some boys who were not particularly bright," he answered, with an amused look. "Perhaps you might compare quite favourably with them."

"Oh, Papa!" she exclaimed; "is that the best you can say about me?"

"I can say that my daughter seems to me to have as much brain as my son, and of as good quality," he replied kindly, refilling her plate as he spoke; "and I very much doubt his ability to put a room in order more rapidly than she can, and at the same time equally well," he concluded.

"Well, it's a sort of womanish work anyhow, — is n't it, Papa?" queried Max, giving Lulu another laughing look.

"I don't see it so," replied his father. "I

would be sorry to admit, or to think, that women have a monopoly of the good qualities of
order and cleanliness."

" I, too, sir," said Max; " and I'm quite resolved to do my father credit in that line as well
as others, at the academy and elsewhere."

" Are we going at once, Papa?" Lulu asked
as they left the table.

" No; but probably in ten or fifteen minutes.
Can you wait so long as that?" he asked, with a
humorous smile, and softly smoothing her hair
as she stood by his side.

" Oh, yes, sir!" she answered brightly. " I
hope I'm not quite so impatient as I used to be;
and I feel quite sure you'll not let Max or me
miss anything very interesting or important."

" Not if I can well help it, daughter," he said.
" I want you and Max to see and hear all that I
think will be instructive, or give you pleasure."

A few moments later they set out; and they
had just reached the grove up by the guard-tents,
and seated themselves comfortably, when the
drum tapped for morning parade, and the cadets
were seen issuing from their tents, buttoned to
the throat in faultlessly fitting uniforms, their
collars, cuffs, gloves, belts, and trousers of spot-
less white, their rifles, and every bit of metal
about them gleaming with polish.

" How fine the fellows do look, Lu!" remarked Max, in an undertone.

"Yes," she replied; "they could n't be neater if they were girls."

"No, I should think not," he returned, with a laugh. "Oh, see! yonder comes the band. Now we 'll soon have some music."

"And there come some officers," said Lulu; and as she spoke the sentry on No. 1 rattled his piece, with a shout that re-echoed from the hills, "Turn out the guard, Commandant of Cadets!" and instantly the members of the guard were seen hastily to snatch their rifles from the racks, form ranks, and present arms.

"Oh, Maxie, is n't that fine!" whispered Lulu, ecstatically. "Would n't you like to be that officer?"

"I 'd ten times rather be captain of a good ship," returned Max.

"I believe I 'd rather be in the navy, too, if I were a boy," she said; "but I 'd like the army next best."

"Yes, so would I."

But the drum again tapped sharply, the cadets in each street resolved themselves into two long parallel lines, elbow to elbow, and at the last tap faced suddenly outward, while the glistening rifles sprang up to "support arms;" every first sergeant called off his roll, every man as he answered to his name snapping down his piece to the "carry" and "order."

That done, the sergeant faced his captain, sa-

luting in soldierly fashion, and took his post; the
captain whipped out his shining sword; the lieutenants stepped to their posts.

"This is the morning inspection," Mr. Keith
said in reply to an inquiring look from Max and
Lulu.

"Are they very particular, sir?" queried
Max.

"Very; should a speck of rust be found on a
cadet's rifle, a single button missing from his
clothing, or unfastened, a spot on his trousers,
a rip or tear in his gloves, or dust on his shoes,
it is likely to be noted on the company delin-
quency-book to-day, and published to the battalion to-morrow evening."

"I wonder if they're as strict and hard on a
fellow as that at Annapolis," thought Max to
himself. "I mean to ask Papa about it."

The inspection was soon over.

"Now," said Mr. Keith, "there'll be a moment's breathing spell, then more music by the
band while the cadets go through some of their
exercises, which I think you will find well worth
looking at."

They did enjoy it extremely, — the music, the
manœuvres of the cadets under the orders now
of the adjutant, and again of the officer in
command.

There followed a half-hour of rest, in which
Mr. Keith introduced his friend, Captain Ray-

mond, to some of the other officers, and they all
had a little chat together.

But as the clock struck nine the cadets were
again in ranks.

"What are they going to do now, Mr. Keith?"
asked Lulu.

"This is the hour for battery drill," was the
reply.

"Ah, I'm glad we're going to see that!"
said Max. "I'd rather see it than anything
else."

"The cadets are dividing and going in different directions," said Lulu. "Some of them seem
to be going down by the river."

"Yes; some members of the senior class.
They are going to what is called the 'sea-coast
battery' at the water's edge, and presently you
will hear the thunder of great guns coming from
there."

"Oh, can we go and look at them?" asked
Lulu, excitedly. "May we, Papa?" turning to
him.

"I think we shall have a finer sight up
here," he replied. "Am I not right, Mr.
Keith?"

"Yes; I think we would better remain where
we are. I would like you to see what daring
horsemen these youngsters are. See yonder are
the seniors in riding-dress, with gauntlets and
cavalry sabres. Watch how easily they mount,

and how perfectly at home they are upon their steeds."

With intense interest and no little excitement Max and Lulu watched and listened to all that followed, — the rapid movements of column, line, and battery, the flash of sabres, the belching of flame and smoke, accompanied by the thundering roar of the great guns, the stirring bugle blasts, the rearing of the horses when brought to a sudden halt. Even the gentlemen showed unmistakable symptoms of interest and excitement.

The hour of battery drill passed very quickly. When it was over the Captain called a carriage, and he, Mr. Keith, Max, and Lulu drove from one point of interest to another, occupying in this way the time till the hour for the boat from Albany to touch at the point. They took passage on it to New York City, where they left it to board a Sound steamer, — a few hours' journey in which would take them to that part of the sea-coast of Rhode Island which had been selected as the summer resort of the family connection.

CHAPTER V.

EARLY the next morning our party landed at
Newport, where they took a carriage for their
sea-side home. It was early when they arrived,
but they found everybody up, and ready with a
joyful welcome, in both that house and the
next two, occupied by the Dinsmores, Travillas,
and Lelands. The delight of all the Raymonds,
from the Captain down to the baby boy, was a
pretty thing to see.

The occupants of the other cottages were present, and rejoiced with them; and from one and
all Cousin Donald received a very warm welcome. They were evidently much pleased to see
him, and soon made him feel quite at home
among them.

They all sat down to breakfast together, almost immediately upon the arrival of the travellers, and lingered over the table in pleasant
chat, talking of what had occurred to one and
another during the absence of the Captain, Max,
and Lulu, questioning Cousin Donald in regard to loved ones more nearly related to him
than to themselves, and laying plans for his and
their own entertainment during his stay among
them.

" I hope," remarked the Captain, " that some naval vessel will come within reach, so that we may have a chance to visit her in your company, Donald."

" Thank you ; I would greatly enjoy so doing," Donald answered. " I suppose a visit from such a vessel is by no means rare in these parts at this time of year."

" No," the Captain replied, glancing through a window looking upon the sea, as he spoke. " Why, there is one in plain view at this moment ! " he cried, starting to his feet.

They all hastily left the table and gathered upon a porch which gave them a good view of the sea and the man-of-war, hardly a mile away.

" My spy-glass, Max, my son, " the Captain said.

" Here, Papa," answered Max, putting it into his father's hand. " I knew it would be wanted."

" Good boy," returned the Captain. " Ah, yes," looking through the glass, " just as I thought. It is the ' Wanita,' Captain Wade, an old friend of mine ; we were boys together in the Naval Academy." His face shone with pleasure as he spoke. " We must visit her," he added, passing the glass to Donald.

Max and Lulu exchanged glances of delight, — Papa was so kind and indulgent they were almost sure he would take them along if he knew they wished to go.

" Not to-day, Levis? I am sure you must be too much fatigued with your long journey," Violet said, with a look into her husband's eyes that seemed to add, " I could not be content to part from you for an hour just yet."

His answering look was as fond as her own.

" No, dearest," he said, low and tenderly, "nor do I intend to go at all without my little wife, unless she absolutely refuses to accompany me ; we will stay quietly at home to-day, if you wish, and perhaps visit the ' Wanita' to-morrow."

It was a bit of private chat, the others being quite engrossed with the ' Wanita,' taking turns in gazing upon her through the glass.

The next moment Lulu was by her father's side, asking in eager beseeching tones, " Papa, if you go on board that war vessel won't you take Max and me with you? "

" I think it highly probable, in case you should both wish to go," he said, smiling at the look of entreaty in her face and its sudden change to one of extreme delight as she heard his reply.

" Oh, Papa, thank you ever so much ! " she cried, fairly dancing with delight. " There's nothing I'd like better; and I hope we can all go."

" You would enjoy it, my dear? " asked the Captain, turning to his wife.

" I would enjoy going anywhere with you, Levis ; and your company is particularly desirable

on a man-of-war," Violet answered with a happy
laugh.

"Thank you," he returned, with a bow and
smile. "We must have them — Wade and his
officers — here too. It will be a pleasure to entertain them."

"Oh, Papa, how delightful!" cried Lulu,
clapping her hands.

"Ah, my child, let me advise you not to be
too much elated," laughed her father; "they may
have or receive orders to leave this port for some
other before our plan can be carried out."

"What plan is it?" "To what do you re-
fer, Captain?" asked several voices; for nearly
every one had now taken a look at the man-of-
war, and was ready to give attention to something else.

The Captain explained.

"Oh, how delightful!" exclaimed Zoe. "Will
it be a dinner, tea, or evening party, Captain?"

"That question remains open to discussion,
Sister Zoe," he returned, with a twinkle of fun
in his eye. "What would you advise?"

"Oh," she said laughingly, "I am not prepared to answer that question yet."

Then the others joined in with proposals and
suggestions, but nothing was positively decided
upon just at that time.

The day was spent restfully in wandering along
the shore, sitting on the beach or the cottage

porches, chatting and gazing out over the sea, or
napping, — most of the last-named being done by
the lately returned travellers.

The little girls of the family, occasionally
joined by Max Raymond and Walter Travilla,
spent much of the day together, rather apart
from their elders, — Lulu most of the time
giving an account of her trip out West and
weeks of sojourn in the town of Minersville,
the acquaintances she had made, and all that
had happened during the stay there, especially of the sad occurrence which so seri-
ously marred the enjoyment of the last days
of their visit, Max now and then taking part
in the narrative.

Both had a great deal to tell about West
Point and Saratoga, and the places of historical interest in their vicinity. Evidently the
trip to the far West and back again, with their
father, had been one of keen enjoyment to
both of them.

So the day passed and evening drew on. The
little ones were in bed, the others all gathered
upon the porches enjoying the delicious sea-
breeze, and the view of the rolling waves, crested
with foam, and looking like molten silver where
the moonbeams fell full upon them.

Every one seemed gay and happy, and there
was a good deal of cheerful chat, particularly
on the porch of the Raymond cottage, where

were Grandma Elsie, Edward Travilla, Donald
Keith, the Captain, with Violet and his older
children, and some of the other young persons.

The sound of approaching wheels attracted
their attention. A carriage drew up in front of
the house, and from it alighted a gentleman in
the uniform of a captain in the navy.

" Wade ! " exclaimed Captain Raymond, hurrying out to meet him. " My dear friend, this is
very kind in you. I had hardly hoped to see
you until to-morrow, and not then without hunt-
ing you up. You are as welcome as this delicious sea-breeze."

" Thanks, Raymond, that's quite a compliment," laughed the other, shaking hands heartily ;
" but I deserve no thanks, as I came quite as
much for my own satisfaction as for yours. I
understand you have been here for some weeks,
but I only heard of it accidentally this morning."

" But it was only this morning I arrived,"
Captain Raymond said in a tone of amusement ;
then, as they had stepped into the midst of the
group upon the porch, he proceeded to introduce
his friend to the ladies and gentlemen composing it.

There followed an hour of lively, pleasant
chat, during which Captain Wade made acquaintance with not only the grown people, but the
younger ones also, seeming to take a great deal
of interest in them, — Max especially, — listening

with attention and evident sympathy as Captain
Raymond told of his son's prospect of soon becoming a naval cadet.

"You have my best wishes, Max," said Captain Wade. "I hope to live to see you a naval
officer as brave, talented, and as much beloved as
your father was, and still is."

Max's eyes sparkled, and turned upon his
father with a look of deepest respect and affection as he replied, "I could ask nothing better
than that, sir, I am sure."

"And I could wish you nothing better than
that you may prove a son worthy of such a
father," returned Captain Wade. "I have known
him since he was a boy of your age, and never
knew him to be guilty of a mean or dishonour-
able act."

"Thank you, sir," said Max, his cheeks flushing, and his eyes again seeking his father's face
with a look of reverence and filial love ; "it is
very kind in you to tell me that, though it's no
news to me that I'm so fortunate as to be the
son of a man any boy might be proud to own
as his father."

"Bravo, Max!" exclaimed Mr. Keith, with a
pleased laugh. "I like to hear a boy talk in that
way of his father, and certainly you have a good
right to do so."

"No boy ever had a better right than Max has
to speak well of his father," remarked Violet,

lightly, but with an earnest undertone in her sweet voice, "and no one is more capable of judging of that than I, who have lived with them both for years."

"And no one could speak too well of Papa," said Lulu, with impulsive warmth, "for there could n't be a better man than he is."

"I should be sorry to believe that, little daughter," he said, putting an arm round her as she stood close at his side. Then he changed the subject of conversation.

A few minutes later Captain Wade took leave, giving all a cordial invitation to return his call by a visit to the "Wanita."

"We had talked of giving you a call to-morrow," said Captain Raymond, "but that would be a very prompt return of your visit."

"None too prompt," returned Wade. "Our time here together, Raymond, is likely to be all too short, and we would better make the most of it."

"So I think," returned the person addressed; "and I hope we shall have the pleasure of seeing you here frequently."

"I think he 's just as nice as he can be," remarked Rosie Travilla, as the carriage drove away with Captain Wade, "and I hope he 'll visit us again soon."

"So do I," said Lulu, "I believe naval officers are the very nicest gentlemen in the world."

"That's rather strong, is n't it?" laughed her father; "and as you have made the acquaintance of only two or three in the course of your life, I fear you are hardly a competent judge."

"And what of army officers, my little lady?" asked Donald Keith, with a good-humoured laugh. "Have you nothing to say for them?"

"Oh, yes, sir!" she said. "I forgot them at the moment, and I do really think they are *almost* equal to the naval ones."

"Almost!" he repeated. "Well, even that is saying a good deal for us if your father is a fair sample of those belonging to the navy."

But it was growing late, and the little party soon separated for the night.

Lulu was nearly ready for bed when her father came to her room to bid her good-night in the old way she liked so much. He took her in his arms with a fond caress, asking, "Does it seem pleasant to be at home — or with the home folks — again?"

"Yes, indeed, Papa," she answered, putting an arm about his neck and laying her cheek to his, "but you are always a great deal more than half of home to me. Oh, I do love you so dearly!"

"And I you, my own darling," her father replied, caressing her again and again.

"I'd rather have you to love me, Papa, than have all the money in the world without you, or with a father that did n't care much about me," she continued.

"Dear child," he said in tender tones, "I value you, and each one of my children, more than words can express. Now I must bid you good-night, for you need all the sleep you can get between this and sunrise."

"Oh!" she exclaimed, "I do hope to-morrow will be clear, so we can go to see the 'Wanita;' or at least that it won't rain. Perhaps it would be all the pleasanter for a few clouds to keep the sun from being so hot on us."

"No doubt," he replied; "but we must take the weather our heavenly Father sends, and be content and thankful."

"Yes, sir, I'll try to do so; but I do hope it will be such that we can go."

"I hope it will, daughter; but if you should have to give up the trip for the time, I hope and expect to see you do so pleasantly, — which you well may, considering that we are very likely to have other opportunities."

"Well, if anything should happen to keep me at home, and I'm cross or sulky about it, I just hope you'll punish me well for my naughtiness," she said so earnestly that he could scarcely refrain from smiling.

"I'm sure that in that case I should punish myself quite as much as you," he said, giving her another hug. "My dear child, if you care

at all for Papa's happiness, — as I am sure you
do, — try to be so good that he will never have
the pain of inflicting any kind of punishment
upon you."

Then he bade her good-night, and left her to
her rest.

Lulu's head was scarcely on the pillow before
she was fast asleep. When she woke, it was already broad daylight. She sprang up and ran to
the window to take an observation of the weather.

"Cloudy, but not raining," she said, half-
aloud. "Just as I'd like to have it, if only it
will keep so, and not turn to actual rain."

With that she began making a rapid toilet,
thinking she would like to take a little run on
the beach before the summons to breakfast;
but when she reached the porch below, the rain
was falling pretty fast.

"Oh, dear!" she sighed, "why could n't it
keep off for a few hours longer?"

"What, daughter, — the rain?" asked her
father's voice close at her side, while his hand
was laid caressingly upon her head.

"Oh, good-morning, Papa!" she returned,
lifting to his a sorely disappointed face. "I
did n't know you were here. Yes, sir, it is the
rain I'm mourning over, — I do so want to visit
that man-of-war to-day; it's really a great disappointment!"

"I'm sorry you should feel it so!" he returned in a sympathizing tone; "but we won't despair yet. I think this is but a passing shower, which will make the trip all the more enjoyable by cooling the air nicely for us. However, should it prove too inclement for our contemplated little jaunt, we must try to remember that our kind and loving heavenly Father orders all these things, and to be patient and content, — more than content, thankful for whatever He sends!"

"I'll try to be content and thankful, Papa; I certainly ought, when I have so many, *many* blessings, and don't really deserve any of them," she answered, putting her hand into his, and letting him lead her back and forth along the porch, which they had to themselves for the time.

"No; that is true of each one of us," he said. "Did you sleep well?"

"Just as well as possible, Papa," she answered, smiling up into his face. "I didn't know anything from the time my head touched the pillow till I woke to find it broad daylight."

"That is something to be very thankful for, daughter, as you will discover should sickness and pain ever give you long hours of wakefulness, such as fall to the lot of many a poor sufferer."

"I hope that time will never come to either of us, Papa," she said; "but I'd rather it would come to me than to you. Oh, it was so hard to

see you suffer that time you were sick here, and
that other time, when Thunderer threw you!"

"Ah, I shall never forget how tenderly affectionate and helpful my children were to me then,"
he said, with a look and smile that made her heart
bound.

Now others of the family began to join them.
Mr. Keith came out upon the porch too, and
after exchanging a good-morning with those
who had preceded him, remarked that it seemed
doubtful if they would be able to take their proposed trip to visit Captain Wade and his man-
of-war.   But by the time breakfast and family
worship were over, the clouds began to scatter;
and in another hour the carriages were at the
door ready to convey them to the wharf, whence
a boat would take them to the "Wanita."

Every one did not care to go that day; the
party consisted of Grandma Elsie, Edward, Zoe,
Rosie Travilla, Evelyn Leland, Mr. Keith, and
the Raymonds, not including the very little
ones, who were left at home in the care of their
nurse.

It was pronounced by all a most enjoyable little excursion.   The weather proved favourable,
clouds obscuring the sun, but no rain falling;
the officers of the "Wanita" were very polite
and attentive, taking them about the vessel, and
showing them everything likely to interest ladies
and children.

They, particularly Grandma Elsie and Violet, were charmed with the perfect neatness everywhere noticeable; the decks, the store-rooms, the magazine and shell rooms, the passages, the engine and fire rooms (into which they took a peep), — indeed, all parts of the vessel shown them, — were most beautifully neat and clean.

The battery, which contained some new guns, seemed to interest Captain Raymond and Mr. Keith more than anything else, while the ladies and little girls greatly admired their brilliant polish.

When they returned to the shore there was still time for a delightful drive before dinner, which they took, — the best hour for bathing coming in the afternoon.

Captain Wade and his officers took dinner and tea with them the next day by invitation. A great interest in the navy had been aroused in the breasts of the young people, and they watched the officers furtively, and listened with attention to all they said that had any bearing upon that subject.

Max was more and more in love with the prospect before him, and quite resolved to make the very best of his opportunities should he be so fortunate as to gain admission to the Naval Academy.

His father had told him he might have this week entirely for recreation, but on the coming

Monday must begin to review his studies preparatory to the examination he would be called upon to pass through at Annapolis.

" I 'm very willing, Papa," he replied. " I 've had a long and delightful vacation already out West with you ; and as I 'm very anxious to pass as good an examination as possible, I want to study hard to get ready for it. And I think it 's ever so kind in you to help me by hearing my lessons."

" Well, my boy," the Captain said, with a pleased look, " make the most of your holidays while they last, though I do not mean that it shall be all work and no play even after this week ; a couple of hours given to study each day will probably be all-sufficient."

" And may I get up early and take them before breakfast when I choose, sir?" Max asked in an eager tone, that told how delightful he would esteem it to be ready to join in the pastimes of the rest of their party, — driving, boating, fishing, bathing, and strolling along the beach and through the woods.

" Yes, my son, if you can manage to get enough sleep in season for that," the Captain replied in an indulgent tone.

" I think I can, sir," said the boy. " I 'll take an afternoon *siesta* if I don't get enough sleep without."

" That will do," said his father. " Remember

health and study must be well attended to, and the more fun and frolic you can manage to get besides, the better I shall be pleased."

Bent on carrying out his plan, Max went early to bed Sunday night, and was up at his books working hard for a couple of hours before breakfast. It still wanted fifteen or twenty minutes of that time when he went down to the porch with his book in his hand.

His father was alone there, looking over the morning paper.

"Good-morning, Papa," Max said. "I am ready to recite whenever you want to hear me."

"Ah! are you, indeed?" the Captain said, taking the book; "then I shall hear this lesson at once."

Max recited very creditably. His father commended him kindly, then said, "I am going in to the city directly after we have had breakfast and family worship, and shall take you with me if you would like to go."

"Thank you, sir; indeed I would!" returned Max, his eyes shining, for he esteemed it one of his greatest pleasures and privileges to be permitted to go anywhere with his father.

"Yes, I think you will enjoy it," the Captain said, smiling to see how pleased the boy was; "I have an errand which I shall tell to no one but Cousin Donald and you. See here," pointing to an advertisement in the paper he had been reading.

"A yacht for sale!" exclaimed Max; "Oh, Papa, are you going to buy it?"

"That is a question I am not prepared to answer till I have seen it, my boy," replied his father. "I shall take you and Cousin Donald, if he will go, to look at it and help me to decide whether to buy it or not."

Mr. Keith joined them at that moment, and was greeted with a pleasant good-morning and shown the advertisement, the Captain telling him that if the yacht proved such as he would like to own, he meant to buy it, and if the plan was agreeable to his wife, to spend the rest of the summer on board, taking his family and friends with him, making short voyages along the coast and perhaps some distance out to sea.

"Taking the opportunity to give my son some lessons in navigation," he added, with a smiling glance at Max.

"Papa! I couldn't ask anything better!" exclaimed Max, hardly able to contain his delight.

"I'm glad to hear it, my boy," his father said. "But now remember that our errand is a secret between us three until we return from the city."

"Then you'll tell Mamma Vi and the rest, sir?" asked Max.

"If I have made the purchase, yes."

The call to breakfast came at that moment and was promptly obeyed.

Max could hardly eat, so excited was he over the prospect of going to the city with his father on so delightful an errand, but he said not a word on the subject.

The coachman had been given his order in good season, and by the time family prayers were over the carriage and horses were at the gate.

" My dear," Captain Raymond said to Violet, " a business matter calls me to the city, but I hope to return in season to take my wife in bathing, or out driving, or wherever she may wish to go."

" Thank you, sir," she said, smiling up into his eyes ; " I 'll try to be ready for either by the time you return. But is not this a sudden move? I had heard nothing of it before."

" Yes, my dear ; but as I am in some haste, I must defer my explanation until I get home again."

" Oh, I don't ask for an explanation," she returned laughingly, as he gave her a hasty good-by kiss ; " you have always been so good since my first acquaintance with you, that I am quite sure you may be trusted."

" Ah ! I 'm much obliged for your good opinion," he answered, with a twinkle of fun in his eye, as he hastily kissed the children, then hurried with Donald and Max to the carriage.

CHAPTER VI.

THE "Dolphin" proved a trim little craft, beautifully finished and furnished, a schooner-rigged sailing-yacht, gracefully modelled and nearly new; but her former owner had died, and the yacht was to be sold as a necessary measure for the settling of the estate.

Max went into raptures over her; and the Captain was evidently pleased, though he said very little as he went about examining every part of her with keen scrutiny.

"Isn't she all right, Papa?" Max at length ventured to ask.

"I think she is, my son," was the prompt, pleasant-toned reply. "What is your opinion, Keith?"

"It exactly coincides with yours, Raymond; and if I wanted, and could afford so expensive a luxury, I think I shouldn't hesitate to make an offer for her."

"We seem to be quite agreed in our estimate of her," said Captain Raymond; "and I shall take your advice."

"You are quite sure of her speed?" queried Keith.

" Yes; I have seen accounts of her in the papers, showing that she is a fine sailer, as I should feel confident she would be, judging merely from her appearance. She is a beautifully modelled, well-built little craft."

"Looks rather small to you after the naval vessels you were wont to command?" queried Donald Keith, with a good-humoured laugh.

"Yes; but quite captivating to a lover of the sea, nevertheless, and as I see she is such to Max, and have no doubt that she will be to the rest of my family, I am about decided to make the purchase."

Max drew a long breath, while his eyes sparkled with pleasure.

They at once sought the agent whose business it was to attend to the sale of the vessel. It did not take long for him and the Captain to come to an agreement; and the " Dolphin " quickly changed owners.

Max was enraptured, his cheeks glowing, his eyes fairly dancing with delight. He managed, with some difficulty, to keep quiet till they were in the carriage again on the way home, then burst out, " Papa, I think it 's just splendid that you 're the owner of such a beautiful vessel ! And I hope to learn a great deal about the proper management of one while we 're sailing round in her."

" I shall try to teach you all I can, my boy,"

was his father's smiling reply; "and your pleasure in the purchase doubles my own."

"Thank you, sir," said Max. "I intend to
pay good heed to your instructions, and learn as
much as possible, so that I may pass a good examination at Annapolis, and do my father credit."

"But, Max, you might do him as much credit
in the army as in the navy; and how you could
resist the fascinations of West Point, I don't
see," remarked Donald Keith, with a twinkle of
fun in his eye.

"Well, sir, I suppose it's because I am the
son of a seaman; love for the sea runs in the
blood,—is n't that so, Papa?"

"Altogether likely," laughed the Captain. "I
have been supposed to inherit it from my father,
and he from his."

Violet, and the other members of the family,
with some of the relatives from the adjacent cottages, were all on the porch as the carriage drew
up in front of the house, and its occupants
alighted.

"Papa! Papa!" shouted little Elsie and the
baby boy, running to meet him.

"Papa's darlings!" the Captain said, stoop-
ing to caress and fondle them; then, taking them
in his arms, he followed Donald up the porch-
steps, Max close in his rear.

"Take a seat, Cousin Donald," said Violet.
"We are glad to see you all back again. I have

been wondering, my dear, what important business you had to keep you so long away from me and your children."

" It was rather important," returned the Captain, pleasantly. "Max," with an indulgent smile into the lad's eager face, "you may have the pleasure of telling where we have been and what we have done."

"Oh, thank you, sir!" cried Max, and proceeded to avail himself of the permission, going into an enthusiastic description of the beautiful "Dolphin," and winding up with the news that Papa had bought her, and expected to take their whole party — or, at least, as many of them as would like to go — coasting along the shores of all the Atlantic States of New England, and for some distance out to sea.

Lulu was dancing with delight, hugging and kissing her father in a transport of joy, before Max's story came to an end.

"Oh, Papa, how good, — how good and kind you are!" she exclaimed. "I don't think anything could be pleasanter than such a trip as that. It 'll be the greatest fun that ever was. And you 'll command the vessel yourself, won't you? I do hope so; for I am sure nobody else could do it half so well."

"What a flatterer my eldest daughter can show herself to be!" he said, with a good-humoured laugh. "Yes, I do expect to take

command of the dainty little craft, — a small
affair, indeed, compared with a man-of-war.
My dear," turning to Violet, "we have yet to
hear from you on this subject. I hope you
approve of your husband's purchase."

"Entirely, Levis. In fact, I am quite as much
delighted as Lulu seems to be," she answered,
smiling up into his face. "What could be more
enjoyable than sailing about in such a vessel,
with a retired naval officer in command? When
am I to see your ' Dolphin'?"

"Yours quite as much as mine, my dear,"
he replied. "You have only to say the word
at any time, and I will take you over to look
at her."

"Oh, will you?" she exclaimed. "Then suppose we all go over this afternoon, and see what
she is like."

"Agreed!" the Captain said; then glancing
round at the eager faces, "How many of you
would like to go with us?" he asked.

He was answered by a prompt and unanimous
acceptance of his invitation. They all wanted to
see that beautiful "Dolphin;" and after a little
discussion of the matter, it was decided that they
would give up the bath for that day, and start
for Newport harbour immediately upon leaving
the dinner-table.

They made a very jovial party, and were delighted with the vessel and the prospect of sail-

ing in her under the command of one so kind and competent as her new owner.

For the next few days Captain Raymond was busy with his preparations for the voyage, — engaging a crew and getting everything on board that would add to the comfort and enjoyment of his family and guests; the ladies also were occupied with theirs, which were not sufficiently great to interfere with the usual pleasures of a sojourn by the sea-side; then one bright morning saw them all on board, — a merry, happy party.

" Where are we going first, Papa? " asked Lulu, when they were fairly under way.

" On a little trial trip along the coast," he answered.

" And then coming back to Newport? " questioned Gracie.

"Possibly," he said, with a smile into the bright, eager face.

" I think I know, though I 'm not right sure," Max said, looking at his father with a rather mischievous twinkle in his eyes, " what Papa is thinking about."

" Do you, indeed ? " laughed his father. " Well, what is it? "

" Well, sir, I overheard Captain Wade telling you he expected the rest of the squadron would be in soon, — in a day or two, I think he said, — and I have a notion it would be a fine sight for

us all, and that my father kindly means to give
it to us."

"Ah, indeed! you seem to have a great deal
of confidence in your father's desire to give
pleasure to you all," laughed the Captain.
"Well, my boy, events may perhaps show
whether you are right."

The three had followed their father to a portion of the deck at some little distance from the
rest of the party, so that their talk was not overheard by them.

"A squadron?" repeated Grace. "What is
that? Oh, it's a good many ships belonging together, — is n't it, Papa?"

"That will answer very well for a definition,
or description," he replied.

"Oh, how glad I am!" exclaimed Lulu,
clapping her hands in delight. "And will they
go through all their manœuvres, Papa?"

"As I am not the admiral whose orders are
to be obeyed, I cannot say exactly what will
be done, my child," the Captain replied. "I
can only say I intend to have you in the vicinity
in season to see all that may be done. Does that
satisfy you?"

"Oh, yes, sir! and I thank you very, very
much!" she said, taking his hand in both of hers
and squeezing it affectionately.

"I too, Papa," said Grace. "I'm sure we'll
enjoy it ever so much."

"I hope so," he answered. "And now can you three keep the secret from the others, that they may have a pleasant surprise?"

"If we can't, or don't, I think we ought never to be told a secret again," exclaimed Lulu, in her vehement way.

"Perhaps you would not be intrusted with one very soon again," her father said; "but," he added, with a look from one to the other of mingled pride and affection, "I feel quite safe in trusting a secret to the keeping of the eldest three of my children. I am quite sure no one of you would tell anything you knew your father wished kept secret."

"No, indeed, Papa!" said Max. "We would certainly deserve to be severely punished, and never trusted by you again, if we should ever so abuse your confidence."

"Just what I think," said Lulu.

"I too," added Grace. "And, Papa, it's so nice and kind in you to trust us!" looking up into his face with a loving smile as she spoke.

"Is it?" he asked, smoothing her hair with fond, caressing hand. "Well, my pet, it is a very great pleasure to me to be able to do so."

At that moment they were joined by Mr. Keith. The two gentlemen entered into conversation; the two little girls ran down into the cabin to see that the maid was making such disposition of their effects as they desired; while Max, joined by Walter Travilla, made the tour of the vessel for perhaps the fiftieth time, — for ever since the purchase, he had spent at least half of every week-day there, learning from his father and others all he could of her different parts and of her management.

Walter, too, had been there again and again, spending hours at a time in climbing about with Max, who took much pleasure in handing over to him the lessons just learned by himself.

The rest of the party were seated on deck enjoying the breeze and the beauties of sea and land, — for the latter was not yet out of sight, though fast receding.

The weather was lovely, every one in the best of spirits, the younger ones full of fun and frolic, and the day passed most enjoyably to all. The evening was enlivened by music from a very sweet-toned piano in the cabin, by singing, conversation, promenading the deck, and gazing out over the water, watching the rise and fall of the waves, and the passing of ships and steamers.

But the day had been an exciting one, especially to the children, and they were willing enough to retire at an early hour. They gathered on deck, each repeated a verse of Scripture, after which they united in singing a hymn, and Mr. Dinsmore led in prayer. Then the good-nights were said, and all the young people, with some of the older ones, retired to their pretty, cosey state-rooms and their berths.

Great was the surprise of nearly everybody when, coming on deck the next morning, they discovered that they were again in Narragansett Bay. There were many exclamations and questions, "How did it happen?" "Whose mistake was it that instead of being away out at sea, we are back at our starting-point again?" These and other like queries were propounded to the owner and commander of the yacht.

He pointed, with a good-humoured smile, to a number of war-vessels lying quietly at anchor at no very great distance.

"The squadron is in, you see; and I thought my passengers would not like to miss the sight of its evolutions, so brought them back to view them. There will be time afterward for a pleasant little voyage along the coast, or where you will."

The explanation was entirely satisfactory to every one, and there was great rejoicing among the lads and lasses.

"What is it they're going to do, Papa?" asked Gracie.

"I have not been let into that secret, daughter," he answered; "but we may find out after awhile by keeping a close watch upon their movements."

"Oh, Papa, you can read their signals, and

tell us what's coming, can't you? Won't you?" exclaimed Lulu.

"Yes, my child, I can and will," he replied. "But there is the call to breakfast, and you need n't hurry through your meal; for they are not likely, for some hours yet, to begin anything you would want to see."

Encouraged by that assurance, no one cared to make undue haste in eating all that appetite called for of the excellent breakfast presently set before them. But an hour later found them all on deck, young and old keeping a sharp watch on every movement of the vessels composing the squadron, several spy-glasses being constantly turned in their direction.

"Ah!" exclaimed the Captain, at length, while at the same instant Max asked eagerly, "Papa, what is it they are doing there on the 'Wanita'?"

"Getting ready for inspection by the Admiral," was the reply. "See, the men have donned their uniforms and are taking their places on the deck. And yonder — do you see? — the Admiral and his staff are pushing off from the flag-ship."

The boatswain's whistle and the roll of a drum were now heard coming from the "Wanita."

"Oh, and is that the executive officer on the bridge of the 'Wanita,' Papa?" asked Max, excitedly. "And what is he doing?"

"Giving an order to the gunner, doubtless to fire a salute in honour of the Admiral."

Before the words had fairly left the Captain's lips, the loud boom of the first gun burst upon the ear.

"Oh, Max, would n't you like to be in that Admiral's place?" queried Walter Travilla; "I would."

"Oh, our Maxie means to be an admiral one of these days; and I 'm sure I hope he will," said Rosie.

"Very good in you, Rosie," returned Max, smiling and blushing; "but I 'm afraid I 'll be an old man before that happens, if it ever does."

"But you may comfort yourself that you can be very useful in maintaining your country's honour without waiting to be made an admiral," remarked Evelyn Leland, smiling pleasantly at Max.

"Yes," he said, returning the smile, "and it *is* a comfort. We 'd any of us feel it an honour to be useful to our country."

"I 'd like to be," remarked Gracie, "if little girls could do anything."

"Little girls are sometimes a very great blessing and comfort to their fathers," the Captain said, smiling down into her eyes while he laid his right hand tenderly on her pretty head, with its sunny curls streaming in the wind.

In the mean while the firing of the salute had gone on, the Admiral and his staff had reached

the deck of the " Wanita," the marines present-
ing arms, and —

" There, what is he going to do now, Papa?"
queried Lulu, — " the Admiral, I mean."

" Inspect the ship," replied her father.

" What for, Papa?" asked Grace.

" To see that every part of it is in perfect
order."

" I 'm sure he will find it so," said Lulu; " for
when we were there and were taken all over it,
every part was as clean and neat as any lady's
parlour."

Captain Raymond now turned away and began
talking with Mr. Keith on some subject that did
not interest the children, but they continued a
close watch of the " Wanita."

The Admiral presently disappeared from the
deck, but at length they saw him there again,
talking with Captain Wade and his officers; then,
in a few moments he and his staff re-embarked
and returned to the flag-ship.

" What 's going to be done now?" asked one
and another.

" Watch, and you will see presently," said
Captain Raymond. " If you do not wish to
miss something, I advise you to keep both eyes
and ears open."

The advice seemed to be promptly followed.
All eyes gazed intently in the direction of the
" Wanita " and the flag-ship.

Presently a signal was shown by the flag-ship which Captain Raymond promptly interpreted for the enlightenment of those about him, — "Abandon ship."

"What does that mean, Papa?" asked Grace.

"Look and see if you can't find out for yourself," he answered in a pleasant tone.

The signal seemed to have caused a commotion on the deck of each vessel belonging to the squadron. Then there was a great splashing of boats into the water, and of other craft which the Captain explained were life-rafts and catamarans; while at the same time men and boys were scampering about with various articles which he said were provisions, nautical instruments, etc., such as would be needed if the ships were really abandoned out at sea.

"But why would they ever do that, Papa?" Grace asked wonderingly. "I should think it would always be better to stay in their ships, would n't it?"

"Not always, daughter. The ship might be on fire, or leaking so badly that she would be in danger of sinking."

"Oh, yes, sir! I did n't think of that," she responded.

"Oh, see!" said Rosie; "they 've all pushed off away from their ships, and the 'Wanita's' boats are ahead of all the others."

"Now what are they going to do, Papa?" asked Lulu.

"I can tell that only when I see the flag-ship's next signal," he replied. "Ah, there it is, and tells them to go round the harbour under sail."

The children watched with interest and delight as the order was obeyed. It was a very pretty sight, but soon came another signal from the flag-ship, which the Captain told them was one of recall; and the boats returned to their ships.

CHAPTER VII.

THE squadron steamed out to sea, the "Dolphin" keeping most of the time within sight of the naval vessels, its passengers being anxious to see more of the evolutions of the men-of-war, and their commanding officer very willing to indulge their wish. They were out simply for pleasure, and were free to turn in any desired direction.

The weather was all that could possibly be wished; and in the evening everybody was on deck except the very little ones, who were already in their nests. The vessels of the squadron were in sight, and all eyes turned frequently in their direction.

"Do you think they'll do anything to-night, Papa?" asked Grace, taking possession of her father's knee, for at the moment he was sitting among the others.

"Who, daughter?" he asked, smoothing her hair with caressing hand.

"Oh, the Admiral and the rest of them on those war-ships. What do they do at such times when they seem to be sailing around just for pleasure?"

"I rather think it is for profit too," he said. "'In time of peace prepare for war.'"

"But how do they prepare for war, Papa?"

"By having sham fights: going through the motions in a way to do harm to no one; firing what we call blank cartridges, — powder but no balls; getting the men so familiar with their guns that they can handle them rapidly and without making mistakes even in the dark. Ah, see! there it comes!" as at that instant a signal-light from the flag-ship shot up several hundred feet into the air, speedily followed by another and another, till the whole sky seemed bright with them; while Captain Raymond, the only one on the yacht who understood the messages, read them off to the others and called their attention to the movements of the ships in prompt obedience to the orders.

"What is that they 're doing, Papa?" asked Grace, presently.

"Arranging themselves in different orders of battle," he replied, and proceeded to explain each movement as it was made.

"It 's ever so nice to see them," she said, "though I do hope they won't ever have to do any real fighting."

"I hope not, indeed," her father said; "but in this wicked, quarrelsome world the only way to secure peace is to show that we are ready for self-defence in case of attack."

"How beautifully and promptly every signal is obeyed!" remarked Grandma Elsie. "It is a sight worth coming a long distance to see."

"Yes, Mamma," said Violet; "and I'm proud of our navy, even though it is so inferior in size to that of England."

"Inferior in size, but in nothing else, I believe, Mamma Vi," said Max, speaking with some excitement. "You know we've whipped the British twice on the sea in spite of their navy being so very much larger than ours."

"Yes, Maxie, I believe I'm as proud of that fact as even you can be," laughed Violet, while his father gave him a look of mingled amusement and pride.

"I think," remarked Edward Travilla, "that from the beginning of our national life our navy has been one to be proud of."

"In which I entirely agree with you," said the Captain. "But the exhibition seems to be over for to-night, and the hour is a late one to find our young people out of bed."

"Must we go now, Papa?" Lulu asked in a coaxing tone which seemed to add, "I hope you will let us stay at least a little longer."

"Yes," he said; "my little girls may say good-night now and go at once."

They obeyed promptly and cheerfully, and before long the others followed their example, till Mr. Keith and the Captain had the deck to themselves.

They lingered there for quite a long while, seeming to have fallen upon some very interesting topic of conversation; but it was suddenly broken in upon by the sound of the flag-ship's drum, instantly followed by those of all the other vessels of the squadron

"Ah, what is the meaning of that, Raymond?" asked Keith, gazing toward the war-ships with keen interest and excitement. "It sounds to me like a call to battle."

"So it is," replied the Captain, — "a night exercise at the great guns, training the men so that they may be ready for all the surprises of a time of war."

Even as he spoke his passengers came hurrying from the cabin, the ladies and young girls wrapped in dressing-gowns and shawls, hastily thrown on to conceal their night-dresses, one and another asking excitedly what was going to be done now. But even as the words left their lips the thunder of cannon burst upon their ears, drowning the Captain's voice when he would have replied.

"Oh, is it war, brother Levis, *really* war?" queried little Walter, in great excitement.

"No, my boy; only a playing at war, I am thankful to be able to say. You may look and listen without fear that any one is to be killed, or even wounded, unless through carelessness."

But the cannon were thundering again, ship after ship firing off whole broadsides at some imaginary foe. At length, however, it was all over, and the passengers of the "Dolphin" re-

turned to their berths to stay there for the remainder of the night.

"Why, we are anchored, are we not, Levis?"
Violet asked of her husband on awakening the
next morning.

"Yes, my dear," he answered; "we are riding
at anchor in Gardiner's Bay. I suspected that
would prove the destination of the squadron, it
being about the best place for naval exercises in
our Northern waters; and it seems I was right.
The squadron is at anchor now at no great distance from us."

"And what do you suppose they will do here?"

"Probably fight some sham battles on sea and
land. Do you care to witness such?"

"Oh, very much! I should greatly prefer
witnessing a sham battle to a real one. But
they won't be likely to begin it immediately, I
suppose?"

"No; I presume we shall have time for a
hearty breakfast first," replied her husband, with
a slight look of amusement. "Don't allow the
prospect of witnessing a battle to spoil your appetite for your morning meal, little wife."

"Oh, no," she answered, with a pleasant laugh.
"I really am not now so much of a child as all
that would come to."

It was not long before she and nearly every
other passenger had sought the deck to take a
look at their surroundings.

They found Gardiner's Bay a beautiful body of
water bounded by islands on nearly every side,
that forming its eastern shore bearing the same
name.   There were a large number of vessels in
the bay, — several sloops, schooners, and a yacht
or two beside the " Dolphin," to say nothing of
the squadron of war-ships.   But all were lying
quietly at anchor, and our friends willingly responded to the call to breakfast.

Yet no one cared to linger at the table ; and
when all had finished their repast they quickly
repaired to the deck to watch the movements of
the squadron.   But for a while there seemed to
be none, the vessels all riding quietly at anchor.

" Dear me ! " Rosie at length exclaimed, " I
wish they 'd begin to do something ! "

" I think they are going to," said Max.   " See,
there 's a boat leaving the flag-ship ; I suppose to
carry a message to one of the others."

" Oh, I 'll go and ask Papa about it ! " exclaimed Lulu.

" About what, daughter ? " asked the Captain's
voice close at her side.

" That boat that has just left the flag-ship,
sir," she answered.   " Do you know where it 's
going, and what for ? "

" I can only conjecture that it carries some
message, probably from the Admiral to the commander of one of the other vessels."

" It 's pulling for the ' Wanita,' " said Max ;

"and see, there are other boats going about from one vessel to another."

"Yes," his father said, "and see yonder are several boats filled with marines, pulling for the shore of Gardiner's Island. Evidently there is to be a sham fight."

"I'm ever so glad it won't be a real one, Papa," said Grace. "It would be so dreadful to see folks killed."

"It would indeed," he answered. "But you may enjoy the show as much as you can, for no one will be hurt unless by accident."

"All the ships seem to be getting boats ready packed with things," remarked Lulu; "I wonder what they are."

"Quite a variety," replied her father, — "great guns, baggage, arms, provisions, and boxes that doubtless contain materials and tools for repairs, compasses, and other articles too numerous to mention. There! the vessels are signalling that they are ready."

"They are getting into the boats!" exclaimed Max, clapping his hands in delight; "and the other fellows that went first to the island seem to be waiting and all ready to fight them."

Every one on the "Dolphin" was now watching the embarkation with interest, the children in a good deal of excitement; it was like a grand show to them.

"Oh, it's a beautiful sight!" said Eva. "How

bright their guns and bayonets are, with the sun shining on them! And there are the beautiful stars and stripes flying from every boat. But they are all in now, — at least I should think so; the boats look full, — and why don't they start?"

"They are waiting for the Admiral's inspection and order," replied Captain Raymond. "Ah, see, there he is on the bridge of the flag-ship, with his field-glass, looking them over. And now the signal is given for them to proceed."

The boats moved off at once in the direction of the island where the marines had preceded them, Captain Raymond's explanations making all their movements well understood by the young people around him, who thought they had never witnessed so fine a sight as the mimic fight that presently ensued, opened by the marines firing a volley of blank cartridges from the shore, which was immediately replied to by the approaching boats with musketry, howitzers, and Gatling guns.

Soon they reached the shore and landed, the marines meanwhile pouring forth an unceasing fire from behind their breastworks.

A fierce battle followed; there were charges and counter-charges, advances and retreats, men falling as if wounded or killed, and being carried off the field by the stretcher-men.

That last-mentioned sight brought the tears to Gracie's blue eyes, and she asked in tremulous tones, "Are they really hurt or killed, Papa?"

"No, darling," he said, pressing the small hand she had put into his, "it is all pretence, just to teach them what to do in case of actual war."

"Oh, I hope that won't ever come!" she exclaimed, furtively wiping away a tear. "Do you think it will, Papa?"

"Hardly," he said; "but it would be the height of folly not to prepare for such a contingency."

"Hurrah!" cried Max, throwing up his cap, "our side's whipped and the other fellows are retreating!"

"Which do you call our side? And do you mean it *is* whipped, or *has* whipped?" asked Rosie, with a laughing glance at the boy's excited face.

But the Captain was speaking again, and Max was too busy listening to him to bestow any notice upon Rosie's questions.

"Yes," the Captain said, "the marines are retreating; the battle is about over. Our side, as Max calls it, you see, is throwing out advance-guards, rear-guards, and flankers."

"What for, brother Levis?" asked Walter.

"To make sure that they have taken the island."

"And what will come next, Captain?" asked Grandma Elsie, who was watching the movements of the troops with as much interest as the children.

"Fortification, doubtless," he replied. "Ah,

yes ; they are already beginning that work. They must fortify the island in order to be able to hold it."

" How, Papa?" asked Grace.

" By throwing up breastworks, digging rifle-pits, planting guns, and so forth. If you watch closely, you will see what they do."

The children — to say nothing of the older ones — watched closely and with keen interest all the movements of the troops until interrupted by the call to dinner.

They had scarcely returned to their post of observation on the deck, having had barely time to notice the completed fortifications, the tents pitched, and the troops at their midday meal, when a tiny strip of bunting was seen fluttering at the flag-ship's main.

Captain Raymond was the first to notice it. " Ah!" he said, " the fun on the island is over, — at least for the present, — for there is the Admiral's signal of recall."

" I 'll bet the fellows are sorry to see it ! " exclaimed Max ; " for I dare say they were going to have some fun there on the island they 've taken.'

CHAPTER VIII.

THINGS were rather quiet for the rest of the day, much to Max's disgust, though at his father's bidding he tried to forget the disappointment in study.

Toward evening Captain Raymond learned something of the Admiral's plans. Two of the vessels were to take possession of a part of the bay set off as a harbour, the others to blockade the entrance.

In reporting the matter to his passengers, "Now," he said, "the preparations will take them two or three days, and the question is, shall we stay to see it all, or turn about and seek entertainment elsewhere? Let us have the opinion of all the older people, beginning with Grandpa Dinsmore," looking pleasantly at the old gentleman as he spoke.

"My preference would be rather for going at once," replied Mr. Dinsmore; "yet I am entirely willing to have the matter decided by your younger people. I shall be quite content to stay on if it seems desirable to the rest of the company."

The vote of the ladies and gentlemen was then taken, when it appeared that the majority were in favour of immediate departure; and the children, though at first disappointed, grew quite reconciled when a little time had been spent in considering what might be seen and done in other quarters.

"I think, Ned," Zoe said to her husband, "that we would better go back to our cottage, because Laurie and Lily are growing fretful, — tired of the sea, I think."

"Very well, my dear, we will do so if you wish it," was the good-natured reply. "Strange as it may seem, I too am quite desirous to make our twin babies as comfortable as possible," he added, with a pleasant laugh.

"I am sorry you should miss the sight of further operations here, Cousin Donald," remarked Grandma Elsie, turning to her kinsman.

"Thank you, Cousin Elsie," he replied; "but though that would be an interesting sight to me, I expect to find almost if not equal enjoyment in a run out to sea or along shore with my friend Raymond in command of the vessel."

"Oh, I think that 'll be just splendid," exclaimed Max, "and that before we get back, Cousin Donald, you 'll be ready to own up that the navy is a more desirable place to be in than the army."

"Perhaps he would n't own up even if he

thought so," remarked Rosie, with a merry look
at her cousin; "I don't believe I should if I
were in his place."

"Possibly I might," he returned, laughingly,
"but I certainly do not expect to fall quite so
deeply in love with a 'life on the ocean wave,'
though I hope to be always willing and anxious
to serve my country wherever and whenever I
may be needed. I think both army and navy
always have been, and always will be, ready to
defend her on land or sea."

"Yes, sir, I believe that's so," said Max.
"And if ever we should have another war, I
hope I'll be able to help defend her."

"I hope so, my boy," the Captain said, regarding the lad with an expression of fatherly
pride and affection.

An hour later the "Dolphin" was sailing
out of the bay, all her passengers gathered on
deck, taking a farewell look at the vessels belonging to the squadron, and on awaking in the
morning they found themselves lying at anchor
in Newport harbour.

They returned to their cottages for a day or
two; then the Raymonds, Grandma Elsie, with
the youngest two of her children, and Donald
Keith, again set sail in the "Dolphin."

The weather was all that could be desired,
every one well and in the best of spirits.

Max was required to devote a part of each day

to study, and recitation to his father, but did not grumble over that, and took great delight in the lessons in practical navigation given him daily by the Captain.

"Papa," he asked one day, " what's the need of a boy going to the Naval Academy when he can learn everything he needs to know on ship-board with a father like you?"

" But he can't," replied the Captain; " how to sail a ship is by no means all he needs to know to fit him to be an officer in the navy."

" Why, what else is necessary, sir?" asked Max, with a look of surprise.

" A number of things which you saw done at Newport and at Gardiner's Bay are quite necessary. He must know how to fight a battle, take charge of an ordnance foundry, and conduct an astronomical observatory; must have a good knowledge of history, be an able jurist and lin-guist, and a good historian, — besides knowing how to manage a ship in calm or storm."

" Whew ! what a lot of things to cram into one head!" laughed Max, with a slightly troubled look on his bright young face.

" Isn't yours big enough to hold it all?" asked his father, with an amused smile.

" I dare say it is, sir," replied Max, " but the difficulty is to pack it all in right. I presume the teachers will help me to do that, though."

" Certainly; and if you follow their direc-

tions carefully you will have no need to fear
failure."

"Thank you, sir. That's very encouraging,"
said Max; "and I am fully determined to try
my very best, Papa, if it was only not to disgrace my father."

"My dear son," the Captain said, a trifle
huskily, and taking the boy's hand in a warm
clasp, "I don't doubt that you intend to do
as you have said; but never forget that your
only safety is in keeping close to Him who
has said, 'In Me is thine help.'"

It was Saturday evening, — the first that had
found them on the broad ocean, out of sight of
land. They were all on deck, enjoying the delicious evening breeze and a most brilliant sunset.

"Papa," Gracie said, breaking a momentary
silence, "what are we going to do about keeping the Lord's Day to-morrow? We can't go to
church, you know, unless you can sail the 'Dolphin' back to land in the night."

"I cannot do that, daughter," he answered;
"but I can conduct a service here on the deck.
How will that do, do you think?"

"I don't know, Papa," she replied, with some
hesitation, blushing and looking fearful of hurt-
ing his feelings; "I s'pose you could n't preach
a sermon?"

"Why not?" he asked, smiling a little at her
evident embarrassment.

"Because you're not a minister, Papa."

"Why, Gracie! Papa's as good as any minister, I'm sure," exclaimed Lulu, half reproachfully, half indignantly.

"Of course he is; I didn't mean that!" returned Gracie, just ready to burst into tears; "I didn't mean he was n't as good as anybody in this whole world, — for of course he is, — but I thought it was only ministers that preach."

"But I can read a sermon, my pet," the Captain said, "or preach one if I choose; there is no law against it. And we can pray and sing hymns together; and if we put our hearts into it all, our heavenly Father will be as ready to listen to us as to other worshippers in the finest churches on the land."

"That is a very comforting truth," remarked Grandma Elsie; "it is very sweet to reflect that God is as near to us out on the wide and deep sea as to any of his worshippers on the dry land."

"You will hold your service in the morning, I suppose, Captain?" Mr. Keith said inquiringly.

"That is what I had thought of doing, sir," was the reply. "Have you any suggestions to make?"

"Only that we might have a Bible class later in the day."

"Yes, sir; that was a part of my programme, — at least I had thought of teaching my own

children, as is customary with me at home; but
if the suggestion meets with favour, we will re-
solve ourselves into a Bible class, each one able
to read taking part. What do you all say to the
proposition?"

"I highly approve," said Grandma Elsie; "I
am sure the day could not be better spent than
in the study of God's Holy Word."

"Nor more delightfully," said Violet.

"I think we would all like it, Captain," Evelyn
remarked in her quiet way.

"I'm sure I shall," said Lulu; "Papa always
makes Bible lessons very interesting."

"That's so," said Max; "I was never taught
by any minister or Sunday-school teacher that
made them half so interesting."

"It is quite possible that your near relation-
ship to your teacher may have made a good deal
of difference, my children," the Captain said
gravely, though not unkindly. "But who shall
act as teacher on this occasion is a question still
to be decided. I propose Grandma Elsie, as the
eldest of those present, and probably the best
qualified."

"All in favour of that motion please say ay,"
added Violet, playfully. "I am sure no better
teacher could be found than Mamma, though I
incline to the opinion that my husband would
do equally well."

"Much better, I think," Grandma Elsie said;

"and I would greatly prefer to be one of his pupils."

" I can hardly consider myself wise enough to teach my mother," said the Captain, colouring and laughing lightly, " even though she is far too young to be own mother to a man of my age."

" But you may lead a Bible class of which she forms a part, may you not?" queried Donald Keith.

" I suppose that might be possible," the Captain replied, with a humourous look and smile.

" I'm sure you can and will, since such is your mother's wish," Grandma Elsie said in a sportive tone, "and so we may consider that matter settled."

" And Mamma's word having always been law to her children, we will consider it so," Violet said. " Shall we not, Levis?"

" As good and dutiful children I suppose we must, my dear," he returned in the playful tone she particularly liked.

Sunday morning dawned clear and beautiful, a delicious breeze filling the sails and wafting the vessel swiftly onward over the sparkling water.

An hour or so after breakfast, captain, passengers, and crew, except the man at the helm, gathered on deck, every one in neat and appropriate dress. The ladies, gentlemen, and children sat on one side, the crew on the other, Captain Raymond standing between. A Bible and a pile

of hymn-books lay on a stand before him, and
Max was directed to distribute the latter. They
were a part of the supplies Captain Raymond
had laid in for the voyage.

A melodeon also stood near the stand, and
Violet, seating herself before it, led the singing
with which the service opened.

The Captain then offered a short prayer, read a
portion of Scripture, a second hymn was sung;
then he gave them a short discourse on the text,
" They hated Me without a cause."

With much feeling and in simple language that
the youngest and most ignorant of his hearers
could readily understand, he described the lovely
character and beneficent life of Christ upon
earth, — always about His Father's business,
doing good to the souls and bodies of men, —
and the bitter enmity of the scribes and Phari-
sees, who " hated Him without a cause." Then
he went on to tell of the agony in the garden, the
betrayal by Judas, — " one of the twelve," — the
mockery of a trial, the scourging and the crown
of thorns, the carrying of the cross and the
dreadful death upon it.

" All this He bore for you and for me," he concluded in tones tremulous with emotion; " con-
strained by His great love for us, He died that
dreadful death that we might live. And shall
we not love Him in return? Shall we not give
ourselves to Him, and serve Him with all our

powers? It is a reasonable service, a glad service, — a service that gives rest to the soul. He says to each one of us, ' Take My yoke upon you, and learn of Me; for I am meek and lowly in heart; and ye shall find rest unto your souls. For My yoke is easy, and My burden is light.'

" Ah, do not refuse or neglect His invitation, for the only choice is between His service and that of Satan, — that malignant spirit whose fierce desire and effort is to drag all souls down to his own depths of sin and misery; and Jesus only can save you from falling into his cruel hands. But He — the Lord of Life and Glory — invites us all to come and be saved, and ' now is the accepted time; now is the day of salvation.' Delay is most dangerous; life is very uncertain. We are sure of no time but now."

He closed the Bible and sat down; and Violet, again seating herself before the melodeon, softly touched the keys and sang in sweet, low tones, but so distinctly that every word reached the farthest listener, —

> " Come to Jesus, come to Jesus;
> Come to Jesus just now, just now;
> Come to Jesus, come to Jesus just now."

Then, at a sign from the Captain, Mr. Keith followed with an earnest prayer; and with another hymn in which all united, the services closed.

Among the crew was one young man in whom the Captain and Grandma Elsie had both come to feel a peculiar interest. He was evidently an American, and possessed of more intelligence and education than the average sailor before the mast. He had listened with close attention to the Captain's discourse, and with a troubled countenance, as Mrs. Travilla had noticed.

" The Holy Spirit is striving with him, I have little doubt," she said to herself. " Ah, if I could but help him to find Jesus, and to know the sweetness of His love ! "

It was not long before the desired opportunity offered. The young man was at the wheel and no one near, while she paced the deck slowly and alone. Gradually she approached, and when close at his side made some pleasant remark about the vessel and the course they were steering.

He responded in a polite and respectful manner.

Then she spoke of the service of the morning, said she had noticed the attention he paid to the Captain's short sermon, and asked in kindest words and tones if he, like herself, was one who loved Jesus, and trusted in Him for salvation from sin and eternal death.

He sighed deeply, then said with emotion,
"No, madam, but — I wish I were."

" But what is to hinder, my friend, since He
says, ' Him that cometh to me I will in no wise
cast out' ? " she asked gently, feelingly.

He was silent for a moment, evidently from
emotion, then said, rather as if thinking aloud
than addressing her, "If I only knew just
how ! "

" He is very near, and His omniscient eye
reads the heart," she said low and feelingly.
" Speak to Him just as if you could see Him, —
as if you were kneeling at His feet, — and He
will hear.

" The Bible says, ' If we confess our sins, He
is faithful and just to forgive us our sins, and to
cleanse us from all unrighteousness.'   Do you
want that cleansing, my friend?"

He bowed a silent assent.

" Then go to Jesus for it," she said. " He, and
He alone, can give it. He shed His blood for us
that ' God may be just and the justifier of him
that believeth in Jesus ; ' for ' the blood of Jesus
Christ His Son cleanseth us from all sin.' "

There was a moment's silence ; then, " I 'd
like to be a Christian, ma'am," he said, " such
as I see you and the Captain are, but — "

The sentence was left unfinished ; and after a
moment's pause, " I should like you to be a better one than I am," she said, " but Jesus only

can make you such. The work is too difficult for any human creature; but Jesus is all-powerful, — 'able to save them to the uttermost that come unto God by Him, seeing He ever liveth to make intercession for them.' Is not that a precious assurance?"

"It is indeed, ma'am, if — if I only knew it meant me."

"You certainly will be one of those of whom it speaks if you 'come unto God by Him;' and He invites you to come: 'Come unto Me all ye that labour and are heavy laden, and I will give you rest.'"

"Could you tell me just how, ma'am, — as if you were pointing out the right road to a traveller, for instance?"

"I will try," she said. "You must remember that He is always near, — close to us, though we cannot see Him; and you may speak to Him as readily, and with as much assurance that you will be heard, as you have been speaking to me.

"He is full of love and compassion, — love so infinite, compassion so great that He was willing to endure all the agony of death upon the cross, and the far greater suffering caused by the burden of the sins of the world and the consequent hiding of His Father's face; therefore He will not cast you out, will not turn away from you, if you come in true penitence and faith.

"Make confession of your sins and plead for

pardon and acceptance as you would if you could see Him while kneeling at His feet; and He will grant it, will forgive all your transgressions and adopt you into His family to be His own child forever."

But others of the passengers were now drawing near, and he had only time to thank her for her kindly interest in him, and promise to think of what she had been saying, before Walter and Max were at her side. calling her attention to a passing vessel.

A very interesting Bible lesson filled up most of the afternoon, both adults and children taking part; and in the evening hymns were sung and conversation held such as was suited to the sacredness of the day.

CHAPTER IX.

A few days longer the " Dolphin " kept on her eastward course, then was headed for the shore of Massachusetts, bound for Boston, where Mr. Keith must leave her, his furlough having now nearly expired. He and his cousins would be sorry to part; but there was no help for it, as Uncle Sam's orders must be obeyed.

The young folks of the party had particularly enjoyed the little trip out to sea, but expected to find a sail along the coast of the New England States quite as much to their taste, particularly as it would give them an opportunity to look upon some of the scenes of incidents in the two wars with England.

They had come in sight of the coast and were all gathered upon the deck.

" That is Scituate, is it not, Captain?" asked Grandma Elsie, indicating a town that had just come into view.

" Yes," he replied, " and I presume you remember the story of the last war with England, connected with it?"

" I do," she answered; " but I presume it would be new to some at least of these young people."

Then entreaties for the story poured in upon her and the Captain from both boys and girls.

" It is but a short one ; and I would prefer to have the Captain tell it," Mrs. Travilla replied.

" Oh, Papa, please do ! " exclaimed Lulu ; and he complied.

" It was, as I have said, during the last war with England that the occurrence I am about to tell of took place. At that time there was a light-house in the harbour kept by a man named Reuben Bates, who had a family of grown-up sons and daughters.

" He and his sons were members of a militia company of the town, and one day during the war they were all absent from home on that business, leaving the light-house in charge of the daughters, Abigail and Rebecca.

" The girls, who were no doubt keeping a vigilant watch for the approach of the enemy, saw a British ship entering the harbour, and conjectured that it was the design of those on board of her to destroy the fishing-boats in the harbour and perhaps burn the town, or at least rob its inhabitants.

" They must have been brave girls, for at once they began to consider what they could do to drive away the would-be invaders.

" I presume Abigail exclaimed, ' Oh, if we could only make them think there were troops ready to defend the town, and so frighten them away!' And very likely Rebecca replied, 'Perhaps we can. If you can play the fife, I'll beat the drum; and if we are hidden from sight they may think there are troops ready to receive them if they come ashore, and so be afraid to land.'

"So they went around behind some sand-hills and played 'Yankee Doodle' in a lively way that had exactly the desired effect.

"The British ship had sent out boats filled with armed men who were pulling for the shore; but on hearing the music of the drum and fife, they evidently concluded that there might be a large force of American soldiers ready to receive them, and thinking 'discretion the better part of valour,' turned about and pulled back to their ship again without attempting to land."

"Oh, was n't that good?" exclaimed Lulu; "I think the fathers and brothers of those girls must have been proud of them."

"Yes, I dare say they were," said Max.

"I wonder what became of them — those girls — afterward?" said Rosie. "Of course they must have been dead and gone long before this."

"No," replied the Captain, "Abigail died only recently at the advanced age of eighty-nine."

"Papa, won't you stay awhile in Boston and take us to see some of the places connected

with Revolutionary times, — Bunker Hill and its
monument, and maybe some others?" asked
Max.

"I shall be pleased to do so, my son, if nothing happens to prevent," was the pleasant-toned
reply. "It is my strong desire to have my
children well-informed in regard to the history
of their own country."

"And ardent patriots too, Papa, ready to defend her to the utmost of their ability should she
be attacked by any other power?" queried Max,
looking smilingly up into his father's face.

"Yes, my son; particularly the boys," replied
the Captain, smiling in his turn at the lad's
enthusiasm.

"Well, there's one of your girls that I am
sure would find a way to help, Papa, — nursing the
wounded soldiers perhaps, or carrying despatches
or something," said Lulu; "perhaps giving information of an intended attack by the enemy,
as Lydia Darrah did."

"I have no doubt you would do all you could,
daughter, and might perhaps be of more assistance than many a man," her father answered
kindly.

"I'm afraid I shouldn't be brave enough to
do such things as that," remarked Grace, with a
look that seemed to say she felt herself quite
inferior to her braver sister; "but I could pray
for my country, and I know that God hears

and answers prayer, — so that would be helping, would n't it, Papa?"

"Yes, my dear child; the Bible tells us a great deal about the power of prayer; ' Call upon Me in the day of trouble: I will deliver thee, and thou shalt glorify Me,' is one of its promises.

"Yes," said Grandma Elsie, " a cry to God, the Ruler of the universe, for help, may accomplish more than any effort on the part of man to do for himself."

" But people must help themselves too, Mamma?" Walter said, half in assertion, half inquiringly.

" Yes, my son, if they can; ' Faith without works is dead,' the Apostle says. The right way is to do all we can to help ourselves, at the same time asking God's blessing upon our efforts."

"As General Washington did," remarked Mr. Keith. "He was a man of both works and prayer, — a blessing to his country, and to the world; in my estimation the greatest mere man that ever lived. ' First in peace, first in war, first in the hearts of his countrymen.'"

" Yes," assented Grandma Elsie, " I like the toast given by some one, — I have forgotten who it was, — ' Washington: Providence left him childless that his country might call him father.' He seems to me to have been as nearly perfect as one of the sinful race of man could be!"

" Yes," responded Captain Raymond; " thoroughly unselfish, just, generous, modest, self-denying and self-sacrificing, charitable to the poor, forgiving, fearless and heroic ; a God-fearing man who sought nothing for himself, but was ready to do or die for his country ; true to her, to his friends, to his God ; a sincere and earnest Christian, — where can a more noble character be found ? "

" I think," said Mrs. Travilla, " he was an instrument raised up and prepared of God for the work that he did in securing to our beloved country the liberties she now enjoys."

" I very much like what Lord Brougham says of him," remarked Violet.

" Oh, can you repeat it, Mamma Vi ? " queried Lulu, eagerly.

" Yes, I think I can," returned Violet, who was blessed with an excellent memory.

" ' It will be the duty of the historian and sage in all ages to let no occasion pass of commemorating this illustrious man ; and until time shall be no more, will a test of the progress which our race has made in wisdom and virtue be derived from the veneration paid to the immortal name of Washington ! ' "

" I like that," said Rosie, her eyes sparkling with pleasure and enthusiasm, " and it 's none the worse for having come from an Englishman."

" Not a bit," assented Keith.

" Mamma, was Washington commander at

the battle of Bunker Hill? " asked Walter. " I ought to know ; but I can't remember just now."

" No, my son," she answered, " it was fought before he reached Boston, — in fact, the very day, June 17, that Congress agreed to his commission as commander-in-chief of all the Continental forces raised, or to be raised ; and on the 21st he set out on horseback from Philadelphia for Boston to take command of the American army encamped there, — or rather around it, the British being in possession of the town itself. News did not fly then as it does in these days, by any means ; and it was not till he arrived in New York, on the 25th, that the tidings reached him.

" The next day he was in the saddle again, pushing on toward the scene of conflict. He reached Cambridge on the 2d of July, and the next day took command of the army, drawing his sword under an ancient elm."

" Why, just think ! " exclaimed Walter, " it took him nearly two weeks to travel from Philadelphia to Boston, while now we could do it in less than two days. No wonder it took so long to fight the British and drive them out of our country ! "

" I think we 'd do it in less than half that time now," said Max. " We could move so much faster, besides raising a great deal bigger army ;

to say nothing of the navy, that I believe has done better in every one of our wars than the land forces. I remember to have read that the army Washington took command of then consisted of only seventeen thousand men, only fourteen thousand five hundred of them fit for duty; that they were without needed supplies of tents or clothing or as much as nine cartridges to a man."

"Yes; it's a wonder Washington was n't completely discouraged," remarked Evelyn. "I think he surely would have been if he had not put his trust in God and the righteousness of our country's cause."

"No doubt it was that which strengthened him for the long and arduous struggle," said Mrs. Travilla. "Washington was, as I said a moment since, a man of prayer; he looked to God for help in the hour of his country's sorest need, and surely his prayers were heard and answered."

"Yes, Mamma," said Rosie; "I remember reading that he would go into the woods to pray privately for his bleeding country and his suffering soldiers; that some one happened to see him alone there in prayer with the tears coursing down his cheeks. Oh, it's no wonder that with such a leader and in so righteous a cause, our arms were victorious in spite of the fearful odds against us!"

"And it was God who gave us such a leader," responded her mother, "and gave him wisdom and courage for his work, and final success in carrying it on to the desired end."

"Wasn't he a member of the Continental Congress before his election as commander-in-chief of the armies?" asked Rosie.

"Yes," replied her mother. "So was Patrick Henry; and he, when asked whom he considered the greatest man in that body, replied, 'If you speak of eloquence, Mr. Rutledge, of South Carolina, is by far the greatest orator; but if you speak of solid information and sound judgment, Colonel Washington is unquestionably the greatest man on that floor.'"

"How long did Washington stay there close to Boston, Papa?" asked Gracie.

"He carried on the siege for eight months, then on the 17th of March, 1776, succeeded in driving the British away."

"Then did he take possession of the town and stay there awhile?"

"He stayed until April, then went to New York, reaching there on the 13th. Soon after he went to Philadelphia to confer with Congress, then back to New York.

"While he was there anxiously awaiting an attack from the British, the Declaration of Independence, just passed by Congress, was sent him.

The troops were quickly paraded, and the Declaration read at the head of the army.

" In the orders of the day Washington said to the troops, 'The General hopes that this important event will serve as a fresh incentive to every officer and soldier to act with fidelity and courage, as knowing that the peace and safety of his country depend, under God, solely on the success of our arms.'

" But I cannot tell you now the whole story of Washington's services to his country in the war for independence, to say nothing of all that he did for her afterward."

"I think we will read about it after we go home to Woodburn," the Captain said.

" Frederick the Great was a great admirer of Washington," remarked Mr. Keith. "He is said to have pronounced Washington's masterly movements on the Delaware the most brilliant achievements recorded in military annals. And Lossing tells us of a portrait of himself which Frederick sent to Washington accompanied by the very gratifying words, 'From the oldest general in Europe to the greatest general in the world.' As for myself, I must say that I think Washington's success, in spite of all the difficulties and discouragements he had to encounter, was something most wonderful, and was given him in answer to prayer, and because he put his trust in God and looked to Him for wisdom and for help."

" He was certainly one of the most unselfish of men," remarked Violet. "What other man would have refused with scorn and indignation, as he did, the suggestion that his army would like to make him a king?"

" Oh, did they want to make him king, and tell him so?" asked Gracie.

" Yes; did n't you know that?" returned Lulu.

"Papa, won't you tell about it?" Grace asked, turning to her father.

" I will, daughter," he answered in a kindly, affectionate tone, and taking in his the hand she had laid upon his knee.

" The battle of Yorktown, which practically secured the independence of our country, was fought in October, 1781, but the treaty of peace was not signed till Jan. 20, 1783; so our armies were not disbanded, and officers and soldiers were sorely tried by their pay being delayed, and feared, not without reason, that they might be disbanded without Congress making proper provision for meeting their just claims.

" Some of the officers began to doubt the efficiency of the Government, and of all republican institutions, and talked among themselves as to whether it might not be better to establish a monarchy instead; and at length one of them was deputed to confer with Washington on the subject.

" He did so, — it seems in writing, — and even ventured to suggest for him the title of king.

" But, as you have just heard, Washington rebuked the writer severely, saying he was at a loss to conceive what part of his conduct could have given encouragement to an address that seemed to him big with the greatest mischiefs that could befall his country; that if he was not deceived in the knowledge of himself, they could not have found a person to whom their schemes were more disagreeable.

" He also conjured the writer, if he had any regard for his country, concern for himself or posterity, or respect for him, to banish these thoughts from his mind, and never communicate a sentiment of such a nature from himself or any one else."

" Did they give it up then, Papa?" Gracie asked.

" Nothing more was ever said about making Washington king," he answered; " but the next December they sent to Congress a memorial on the subject of their pay. A resolution was adopted by that body, but such as did not satisfy the complainants. Then a meeting of officers was arranged for; and anonymous addresses, commonly known as the Newburg addresses, were sent out to rouse the army to resentment.

" Washington insisted on attending the meeting, and delivered an impressive address.

" He had written down what he wished to say, and after reading the first paragraph paused to put on his spectacles, saying most touchingly, as he did so, that he had grown gray in the service of his country, and now found himself growing blind.

" He then went on to read a most noble paper which he had prepared for the occasion. In it he acknowledged the just claims of the army against the Government, and assured them that they would not be disregarded ; then he entreated them ' to express their utmost horror and detestation of the man who wishes, under any specious pretences, to overturn the liberties of our country, and who wickedly attempts to open the floodgates of civil discord and deluge our rising empire in blood.'

" Then, having finished his address, he retired from the meeting ; but resolutions were at once offered by General Knox, seconded by General Putnam and adopted by the meeting, agreeing with all he had said and reciprocating his expressions of esteem and affection. They were relieved of their doubts and fears and restored to their wonted love for their country."

" Oh, that was nice, Papa ! " exclaimed Gracie, her cheeks flushing and her eyes shining. " How good and great our Washington was ! It seems to me we would never have got free from Great Britain if we had n't had him to help."

" Yes ; it does seem very doubtful," her father replied. "As Grandma Elsie has said, God seems to have raised up and prepared him for that very work."

" And how soon after that was the war really over, Papa?"

" The treaty of peace was signed in Paris on the 20th of January, 1783, as I remarked a moment since ; but as it took a long while in those days for people and news to cross the ocean, it was not till the 17th of the following April that Washington received the proclamation of Congress for the cessation of hostilities. Then on the 19th — which, as you may remember, was the eighth anniversary of the battle of Lexington, the opening conflict of the war — the cessation was proclaimed at the head of every regiment."

" What joyful news it must have been to the poor, weary soldiers ! " said Violet. " I trust their hearts were full of gratitude to God, who had prospered the right in spite of the fearful odds against those who were battling for it."

" Yes," returned her husband ; " and no heart could have been more thankful than that of the commander-in-chief, who said in the general orders, ' The chaplains of the several brigades will render thanks to Almighty God for all His mercies, particularly for His overruling the wrath of man to His own glory, and causing the rage of war to cease among the nations.' "

" What a good, good Christian man Washington was, Papa ! " exclaimed Gracie.

" And yet he had enemies ; and there are still some among his own countrymen who are far from appreciating him, — can even speak evil of him. But even our Lord Jesus Christ had enemies and detractors — bitter and implacable foes — among his own countrymen ; and ' the servant is not greater than his Lord,' " was the Captain's reply.

" Yes, Papa, I remember that Washington had enemies, — Gates for one, and that infamous Conway for another," said Max. " How glad I was to read of the Continental Congress accepting the resignation he offered in a fit of anger, so that he had to leave the army for good, though he did n't want to ! "

" I think it was for good, Max," remarked Mr. Keith, with a slightly amused smile, — " for the good of the country, though perhaps not for his own. Conway was a man America was well rid of ; and the same may be as truly said of Charles Lee. What would have become of our liberties had that infamous cabal succeeded in getting the command taken from Washington and given to any one of themselves ! "

CHAPTER X.

EVELYN LELAND was the only one of the party on the " Dolphin " who had never seen Boston ; but to all the young people entering the city from the sea was a new experience, and as the vessel neared the harbour they gazed about them with great interest, while the Captain pointed out and named the forts and the islands as they came into view.

" Yonder is Boston Light," he said, " two miles east of Fort Warren, — on George's Island, which I will point out presently ; it is a revolving light, ninety-two feet above the level of the sea. And yonder is Spit or Bug Light ; it is only thirty-five feet high, and stands upon iron pillars fixed in the rock. They show a red fixed light there which can be seen at the distance of seven miles.

" Then there is Long Island Light, named from the island on which it stands. The tower is only twenty-two feet above the ground, but eighty feet above the sea.

" Yonder," again pointing with his finger, " is Fort Independence (called in Revolutionary times Castle William) just at the entrance of the main channel ; and opposite it is Fort Winthrop.

And yonder is George's Island with its fortification, — Fort Warren."

" And this was the harbour where the Boston
Tea-party was held ! " remarked Evelyn, in a half-
musing tone. " What an exciting time that
must have been ! I think it was grand in the
people to give up the tea they so enjoyed drinking, rather than submit to ' taxation without
representation.' "

" Which all women possessed of landed property
do to this day," returned Rosie, mischievously.

Eva laughed. " Oh, well," she said, " you
know American women can influence the voters
to whom they are related, — their brothers, hus-
bands, and sons."

" If they have any, and they happen to be
particularly tractable," laughed Rosie. " But
how about poor fatherless and brotherless single
women ? The men may vote as heavy taxes
upon their property as they please, while they
can't lift a finger to prevent it, or say a word
as to what is to be done with the money taken
from their purses without their consent."

" Why, Rosie, are you turning into a woman's
rights woman ? " queried Max, laughing.

" I don't know, Maxie ; those ideas just happened to suggest themselves," she answered.
" I 'll take time to think it all out one of these
days, though ; and I 'll not promise not to turn
into an advocate of women's right to have some

say about the taxing of their own property. I
see no reason why a man's rights in that direction
should be considered superior to a woman's."

" No ; nor I either," Max said. " And I'm as
willing as possible that American women should
have all their rights ; but I should n't like to let
ignorant women — foreign or coloured ones —
vote."

" Yes, that 's the trouble," laughed Rosie ; " I
should n't like that either. But I can't see that
it 's any better to let foreign *men* who are too
ignorant to understand much or anything about
our institutions, have a vote. I must say it
strikes me as exceedingly insulting to educated,
intelligent ladies, who are native Americans, to
refuse a vote to *them*, and at the same time give
it to *such foreign-born men*, or to male natives
who know nothing, can't read or write, and have
no property at all."

" Coloured men, for instance?" queried Max.

" Yes, coloured or white ; it 's the education
I 'm concerned about, not the colour. Mamma,
do not you agree with me?"

" Yes, I do," Mrs. Travilla answered. " I
have no desire to vote myself ; but I think only
native-born citizens, or those who have been
twenty-one years in the country, should have a
vote, and not even they unless able to read and
write, capable of understanding our form of government, and possessed of some little property, —

that last in order that they may appreciate more fully the burdens of taxation, and be less ready to make them heavier than need be."

" Papa," asked Gracie, " where abouts were the tea ships when the folks went on board and threw the tea into the water?"

" They were moored at Griffin's Wharf," he replied; " I can point it out to you directly."

" What is it, Papa, Gracie's talking about? A story?" queried little Elsie. " Please, Papa, tell it to us."

" I'm afraid you would hardly understand, Papa's darling," the Captain said, stroking the soft, shining, golden curls as he spoke, and smiling down into the bright, eager little face.

" I think I should, Papa. Wasn't it something 'bout a tea-party?" she asked coaxingly.

" Yes, Papa, please do tell the story; we'd all like to hear it over again now when we're just at the place where it happened," added Gracie.

" Well, my darlings, to please you," he said; " also because I want you to be thoroughly grounded in the history of your own country.

" You must remember that these States, — or rather the original thirteen, there were only so many at that time, — were then called colonies, and were ruled by England. The English Government claimed the right to tax the colonies just as they pleased. That right the people of the colonies denied.

" They were not allowed to send any members
to Parliament to help decide who in America
should be taxed and how much ; so they determined that rather than pay a tax put upon the
article without their knowledge and consent,
they would do without tea.

" Then the English Government tried to force
it on them ; and these ships came into their harbour loaded with the tea, which they intended
to land.

" One of those tea-laden ships, called the
'Dartmouth,' — Captain Hall in command, —
came to anchor yonder, near the Castle, as it
was then called. It was on Sunday the 'Dartmouth' came in ; and as you may suppose,
the sight of her caused a great excitement in
Boston.

" Early on Monday morning a placard was
posted all over the town. I committed it to
memory when a school-boy. It said : —

" ' Friends ! Brethren ! Countrymen ! That worst
of plagues, the detested tea shipped for this port by
the East India Company, is now arrived in the harbor ;
the Hour of Destruction, or manly opposition to the
Machinations of Tyranny, stares you in the face ;
every Friend to his Country, to himself, and to Posterity, is now called upon to meet at Faneuil Hall, at
nine o'clock This Day (at which time the bells will ring),
to make united and successful resistance to this last,
worst, and most destructive measure of administration.'

" That was the handbill ; its date was November 29, 1773."

" Was that the 'vite to the tea-party ? " asked little Elsie.

" Not to what proved to be the principal one," he answered.

" In response to the call they met that day at Faneuil Hall, but the excitement was so great and brought so many people together that they adjourned to the Old South Meeting-house which was larger.

" At that meeting it was resolved that the tea should not be landed, that no duty should be paid on it, and that it should be sent back in the same vessel it had come in ; also they notified the owner and the commander of the vessel that to land and enter the tea was at their own peril, ordered the ship to be moored at Griffin's Wharf, and appointed a guard of twenty-five men to watch her.

" At the meeting a letter was received from the consignees offering to store the tea till they could hear from England ; but the people were determined not to allow it to be landed, so rejected the offer with scorn.

" Then the sheriff read a proclamation from the governor ordering them to disperse ; but it was received with hisses, and they went on with the business that had called them together.

" They passed a resolution ordering the vessels

of Captains Coffin and Bruce, which were hourly
expected to arrive with their loads of tea, to be
moored at Griffin's Wharf."

" Did they come, Papa? and did the men
watch all the ships that had tea?" asked Elsie,
who was listening with a look of interest and intelligence that seemed to say she understood a
great deal, if not all her father had been
saying.

" Yes ; and about two weeks afterward
another meeting was held in the Old South
Church, when it was resolved that Mr. Roch
must immediately apply for a clearance for his
ship and send her out to sea again. But the
governor had already taken measures to prevent him from doing that, ordering Admiral
Montague to fit out two armed vessels and station
them at the entrance to the harbour, and Colonel
Leslie, who was in command of the Castle, not to
allow any vessel to pass out under the guns of
the fortress, unless she could show a permission
signed by himself."

" I should think," remarked Max, " that Mr.
Roch and Captain Hall must have been quite
puzzled to know how to act to suit all parties."

" What happened next, Papa?" asked Gracie.

" Two days later there was another meeting in
the Old South, — the largest meeting that had
then ever been known in Boston ; for the people
were greatly excited.

"Several persons made addresses, but Josiah Quincy was the principal speaker. He advised the people to weigh and consider before they took measures that would bring on a trying and terrible struggle such as had never been seen in this country."

"Why, Papa," exclaimed Lulu, "I thought Mr. Quincy was one of the patriots!"

"So he was, my child; but he wanted the people to look before they leaped.

"When he had finished his speech the question was put, 'Will you abide by your former resolutions with respect to not suffering the tea to be landed?'"

"And what did they say?" asked Gracie.

"That they would; the whole vast assembly speaking as with one voice."

"I hope Mr. Roch was there to hear them," said Lulu.

"No," said her father. "The governor was at his country-house, a few miles out of Boston, and Mr. Roch had been sent to him to ask a permit for his vessel to leave the harbour.

"He returned late in the afternoon, before the meeting at the Old South had broken up, and reported to them that the governor refused a permit until a clearance should be shown him; and the collector refused that until the tea should be landed."

"What a fuss about nothing!" exclaimed little Elsie, with a look of disgust.

"Oh, no," her father said, stroking her hair as she leaned upon his knee; "some day when my little girl is older and wiser, she will understand that it was very far from being about nothing.

"The people were very much excited. It was beginning to grow dark in the old church and somebody called for candles; but just then somebody in the gallery showed himself disguised like a Mohawk Indian, raised the Indian war-whoop, and was answered in the same fashion by some one outside the building, — for the throng a good deal more than filled the church; then another voice in the gallery shouted, 'Boston harbour a teapot to-night! Hurrah for Griffin's Wharf!'

"At that there was an instant motion to adjourn, and the people crowded into the streets.

"It was a clear, moonlight evening, still quite early, and the British squadron not more than a mile away; British troops were near too, but neither interfered with what was going on.

"It is probable that everything had been arranged beforehand; and seeing several persons disguised as Indians going toward Griffin's Wharf, the people hurried thither. Some fifteen or twenty were so disguised, but about sixty boarded the vessels in the first place; and it is said that as many as a hundred and forty were engaged in the work before it was finished.

"A man named Lendall Pitts acted as leader; and under his direction the 'Dartmouth' was boarded first, the hatches were taken up, and her cargo of one hundred and fourteen chests of tea brought on deck, where the boxes were broken open and the tea was thrown into the water.

"Then the other two vessels were boarded and their cargoes of tea also thrown into the harbour."

"And that's what is called the 'Boston Tea Party,'" remarked Max with satisfaction. "I'd wish I'd been there to help, only that I'd rather be here now."

"That's just the way I feel about it," said Walter.

"You may be thankful, my dear boys, that you live in these days," remarked Grandma Elsie, smiling kindly upon them. "War times are more interesting to tell about, but far harder to live in. Our hearts may well be filled with thankfulness to God for the success of our fathers in securing the blessings of liberty for not themselves only, but for us also. We assuredly have more to be thankful for than any other nation, and ought therefore to be better and more earnest Christians, doing all we possibly can to spread abroad through all the earth the glad news of salvation by Christ, and to help the down-trodden and oppressed to share with us the inestimable blessings of freedom, — life, liberty, and the pursuit of happiness, as our Declaration of Independence has it."

But the " Dolphin " was fast approaching the city, and there was so much to look at and talk about, relating to the present, that for a time the past was well-nigh forgotten, except when the Captain pointed out as nearly as he could, the precise spot where the never-to-be-forgotten " tea party " had been held.

When he had done so, Max broke out into a song to the tune of " Yankee Doodle," the other young folks joining in with a will on the chorus.

" Once on a time old Johnny Bull flew in a raging
    fury,
  And swore that Jonathan should have no trial, sir,
    by jury;
  That no elections should be held across the briny
    waters ;
  And now said he, ' I 'll tax the Tea of all his sons
    and daughters.'
  Then down he sate in burly state, and blustered like
    a grandee,
  And in derision made a tune called ' Yankee Doodle
    Dandy.'
    Yankee doodle, — these are facts, — Yankee doodle
      dandy!
    My son of wax, your tea I 'll tax ; you — Yankee
      doodle dandy!

"John sent the tea from o'er the sea, with heavy
    duties rated;
But whether hyson or bohea I never heard it stated.
Then Jonathan to pout began, — he laid a strong
    embargo, —
'I 'll drink no Tea by Jove!' so he threw overboard
    the cargo.
Then Johnny sent a regiment, big words and looks
    to bandy,
Whose martial band, when near the land played
    'Yankee Doodle Dandy.'
    Yankee doodle, — keep it up, — Yankee doodle
        dandy!
    I 'll poison with a tax your cup; *you* — Yankee
        doodle dandy!

"A long war then they had, in which John was at last
    defeated;
And 'Yankee Doodle' was the march to which his
    troops retreated.
Cute Jonathan, to see them fly, could not restrain
    his laughter;
'That time,' said he, 'suits to a T. I 'll sing it ever
    after.'
Old Johnny's face, to his disgrace, was flushed with
    beer and brandy,
E'en while he swore to sing no more this 'Yankee
    Doodle Dandy.'
    Yankee doodle, — ho, ha, he, — Yankee doodle
        dandy!
    We kept the tune, but not the tea; Yankee doodle
        dandy!

" I 've told you now the origin of this most lively
  ditty,
Which Johnny Bull dislikes as 'dull and stupid' —
  what a pity!
With ' Hail Columbia ' it is sung, in chorus full and
  hearty.
On land and main we breathe the strain John made
  for his ' tea party; '
No matter how we rhyme the words, the music
  speaks them handy,
And where 's the fair can't sing the air of ' Yankee
  Doodle Dandy' ?
  Yankee doodle, firm and true, — Yankee doodle
    dandy !
  Yankee doodle, doodle do, Yankee doodle dandy! "

CHAPTER XI.

A few days were spent in Boston, principally in visiting places of historical interest, — Christ Church on Salem Street, where as the Captain told the children, Paul Revere's signal was hung out from the steeple, in the Revolutionary War, by Captain Pulling, a Boston merchant; and the Old South Church, about which they had already heard so much.

"In 1775," the Captain said, as the little group stood gazing about it in deep interest, "the British soldiers desecrated this place by using it for cavalry drill, having first torn out the galleries and covered the floor with earth. It is now no longer used as a church, but, as you see, is a historical museum. Now we will go to Faneuil Hall, — 'the cradle of liberty.'"

They did so; and next visited the Old State House.

As the Captain told them, the Boston Massacre occurred in the street before it; and there, during the excitement in regard to the Stamp Act, the stamped clearances were burned by the mob. From the balcony the Declaration of Independence was read. Many town-meetings were held there, and many patriotic speeches made, — among them those of Otis, who foretold probable war, and urged resistance to tyranny " even unto blood" if necessary.

" Who was Otis, Papa?" asked Lulu.

" A Boston lawyer of that time, a patriot, — as evidenced by even the few words of his I have just quoted. He was advocate-general with a good salary at the time when the revenue officers in Boston took out search-warrants to look for smuggled goods, and called upon him to defend their cause ; but he at once resigned his office and took the other side, — that of the merchants of Boston, who were protesting against the writs. They offered him a large fee, but he refused it, saying, ' In such a cause I despise all fees.' "

" That case was tried in this old State House ; and Otis made a grand speech of such length that it took him five hours to deliver it."

" What was it all about, Papa?" asked Gracie.

" It was on the question whether Americans were bound to obey laws which they had no share in making, and all the arguments in the wonderful speech answered doggedly, ' No.'

" John Adams, who heard the speech, afterward said that on that day ' the child Independence was born;' and no doubt the argument assisted the popular leaders very much in furnishing them with weapons for their work."

"Weapons, Papa?" Grace asked with a puzzled look.

"Yes, daughter; arguments with which to show the people what the English Government was doing to take away our liberties.

"Otis afterward, when Governor Bernard called upon the General Assembly of Massachusetts to rescind the resolution it had passed against the right of the English Parliament to tax the colonies without their consent, — which they boldly disregarded, — made a powerful speech in which he said, 'When Lord Hillsborough knows that we will not rescind *our* acts, he should apply to Parliament to rescind *theirs*. *Let Britons rescind their measures, or they are lost forever!*' He went on speaking in that way for nearly an hour, till even the Sons of Liberty began to tremble lest he should go too far, and be charged with treason."

"And did he fight for the country, Papa?" asked Gracie.

"No, poor fellow!" replied the Captain, with a slight sigh; "before the war had fairly begun he became insane from injuries inflicted by one Robinson, a commissioner of customs, who, with several army or navy officers set upon, beat, and otherwise injured him, inflicting a sword-cut on his head from which he never recovered."

"And he did n't have the pleasure of seeing

his country free and separated from England?" Lulu said, half inquiringly.

" No ; he was killed by a stroke of lightning in 1778, which you will remember was several years before the war was over."

Our little party next visited Lexington and Concord.

" How far must we travel to get there, Papa?" queried Gracie, as they took their seats in the car.

" Only a few miles to Lexington, and a little farther to reach Concord," he answered.

" That won't seem very far by rail," remarked Max ; " but it must have seemed quite a distance to the soldiers who marched there in Revolutionary times."

" I find we are early," the Captain said, looking at his watch ; " and as we have the car nearly to ourselves, it may be well for us to talk over what occurred in 1775 at the places we are about to visit. I think it will make the visit more in, teresting to you."

" Oh, do tell us the whole story, Papa," requested Gracie, with a look of pleased anticipation.

The others all joined in her petition, and the Captain good-naturedly complied.

" Matters had been growing worse and worse between the British Government and the colonies," he said, " till a struggle seemed almost inevitable. General Gage discovered that the patriots were privately conveying arms out of Boston, that some brass cannon and field-pieces were at Salem ; and on a Sunday in February, 1775, he sent some troops to seize them.

" An express from Marblehead arrived at Salem while the people were in church, with the news that British troops were landing from a transport at that place, and were about to march to Salem.

" The congregations were at once dismissed, and, led by Colonel Pickering, stopped the British at a drawbridge. Pickering succeeded in effecting a compromise, and the troops marched back again to Marblehead without having done the errand upon which they had been sent.

" Let me see," continued the Captain, meditatively ; " I think I can recall some lines by Trumbull, referring to that incident : —

" ' Through Salem straight, without delay,
   The bold battalion took its way;
   Marched o 'er a bridge, in open sight
   Of several Yankees arm'd for fight ;
   Then, without loss of time or men,
   Veer'd round for Boston back again,
   And found so well their prospects thrive,
   That every soul got back alive.'

" It was some two months after this that the battles of Lexington and Concord took place. On April 18, the patriots learned that the next day British troops were to visit Concord for the purpose of destroying some military stores there, and passing through Lexington seize the persons of John Hancock and Samuel Adams, who were both in that town at the house of the Rev. Jonas Clark.

" Gage had tried to keep all this a profound secret, but somehow the patriots had learned what he was attempting, and were making their preparations accordingly. Warren and his friends had gone, Paul Revere and William Dawes had just rowed across the river to Charlestown, taking a message from Warren to Adams and Hancock. They were very near being captured by the guard at Charlestown, but escaped, and reached Lexington a little after midnight.

" They went at once to Mr. Clark's house, but found a guard of eight minute-men placed about it to protect Adams and Hancock.

" These refused to let Revere and Dawes into the house, as orders had been given not to allow the inmates to be disturbed by noise.

" ' Noise ! ' exclaimed Revere, ' you 'll have noise enough before long ; the regulars are coming ! '

" They were quickly admitted then, roused Hancock and Adams, and knowing how unlikely to escape being taken prisoners they were, should they remain in Lexington, persuaded them to retire to Woburn.

"Then Revere and Dawes pushed on to Concord to give the alarm there.

"By two o'clock in the morning a hundred and thirty of the Lexington militia were collected at the meeting-house upon the green. The roll was called; then, as the early morning air was very chilly, they were dismissed with orders to remain within drum-beat."

"Papa, the British marched very quietly, did n't they?" asked Max.

"Yes, in perfect silence; hoping and believing that none of the Americans were aware of their movements."

"Ha, ha, how mistaken they were!" laughed Max.

"Yes," his father said, "there were vigilant eyes upon them. As they passed through West Cambridge they were seen by Lee, Gerry, and Orne, — members of the Provincial Congress, — and as I have told you, others learned the secret also.

"As the British neared Lexington their ears were greeted by the sound of bells and guns, warning them that their expedition was known."

"I s'pose they did n't like that," observed Gracie, "but what did they do about it, Papa?"

"Colonel Smith dispatched six companies of troops under Major Pitcairn, with orders to press on to Concord and secure the two bridges.

He also sent a messenger to Boston for reinforcements.

" Pitcairn hastened on toward Lexington, capturing several persons on his way.   One of them — a man named Bowman — escaped, hurried into Lexington on horseback, and notified Captain Parker, commander of the minute-men, that the enemy was approaching."

" And did they make a great fuss and wake up all the people, Papa? " asked Gracie.

" They rang the bells, fired guns, and beat the drum, so that doubtless everybody was soon aroused.

" It was between four and five in the morning. About one hundred of the militia were quickly collected on the green ; but being raw troops, and uncertain how large a force was coming against them, they were in some confusion.

" And indeed it was an overwhelming force they presently saw marching toward them, their scarlet uniforms gleaming out through the early morning mist.

" The British halted within a few rods of the meeting-house and loaded their pieces.   But the Americans stood firm and undismayed.

" Their orders were not to pull a trigger till fired upon by the enemy, and for a moment there was silence and hesitation on both sides ; neither Americans nor British seemed willing to become the aggressors.

" But it was only for a moment ; Pitcairn and other officers galloped forward, waving their swords over their heads, and followed by their troops in double-quick time.

" ' Disperse you villains ! ' they shouted, ' lay down your arms and disperse. Why don't you disperse, you rebels? Disperse ! ' And as the patriots did not instantly obey the command, Pitcairn wheeled his horse, waved his sword, and gave orders to press forward and surround the militia.

" At that instant some random shots were fired by the British, and promptly returned by the Americans."

" Oh, Papa, was anybody killed ? " asked Gracie.

" Not by those shots," replied her father ; " but the next minute Pitcairn drew a pistol and discharged it, at the same time shouting ' Fire ! '

" His troops instantly obeyed that order. Four of the patriots were killed, and the rest dispersed. They were fired upon again while retreating, and several of them halted and returned the shots, then concealed themselves behind buildings and stone walls.

" Eight Americans were killed, three British soldiers and Major Pitcairn's horse were wounded."

" I thought you said only four Americans were

shot, Papa," said Gracie, looking up inquiringly into his face.

" Four by the first discharge of musketry, and as many more while trying to escape over the fences," he answered.

" Did the British care for having killed those poor men?" she asked, tears of sympathy shining in her eyes.

" If so they gave no evidence of it," her father replied. " They hurried on to Concord in high spirits. But the news of their approach had been communicated, and a formidable body of militia was waiting to receive them."

" Oh, yes!" said Rosie, "I remember that Dawes and Revere had hurried on to warn them after doing the Lexington people the same service."

" Yes," the Captain said, " but on the way they were taken prisoners by some British officers. They had stopped to tell the news to Dr. Samuel Prescott, who escaped over a wall, they being captured. Prescott made his way to Concord, reaching there about two o'clock in the morning, and gave the alarm. Then the bells were rung, and the people armed themselves, so that before daylight they were ready to receive the British."

" They knew what the British were after, and made haste to conceal the stores of powder, shot, and so forth, — did n't they, Papa?" asked Max.

"Yes; the whole male population and some of the women assisted in that work, and succeeded in concealing them in a safe place in the woods before the arrival of the British."

"That was good," remarked Gracie. "And did n't the British get anything at all, Papa?"

"Yes, a little. They knocked off the trunnions of three iron twenty-four-pound cannon, cut down a liberty-pole, set the Court House on fire, and burned a few barrels of wooden trenchers and spoons, and sixteen new carriage-wheels. Also they threw five hundred pounds of balls into a mill-pond, and broke open about sixty barrels of flour; but the people succeeded in saving a good deal of that, and Mrs. Moulton put out the fire in the Court House before much damage was done."

"But was there no fighting, Papa?" Gracie asked.

"There was fighting," the Captain answered. "While the British were at the mischief I have been telling you of, the American party was rapidly increasing by the coming in of minutemen from the neighbouring towns. They formed into line as fast as they came. There were nearly four hundred of them.

"From the place where they were forming they could see the fire the British had started in the centre of the town, and of course the sight greatly increased their excitement.

" Joseph Hosmer, the adjutant, made a stir-ring appeal, after a brief consultation with prominent citizens and members of the Committee of Safety, who were present, and ready to take part in repelling the British.

" It was agreed to dislodge them from the North Bridge. Captain Davis saying, ' I have n't a man that 's afraid to go.'

" They wheeled into marching order, and joined by other companies, pushed forward to the bridge, under the command of Major John Buttrick, of Concord.

" The British guard were on the west side of the river, but crossed to the east on seeing the Americans approaching, and began taking up the planks of the bridge.

" Major Buttrick called to them to stop, and urged his men on to try to save the bridge.

" The British formed for action as the Americans drew near, and some of the regulars fired, killing Captain Davis, Abner Hosmer, and wounding another man.

" Then Buttrick shouted, ' Fire fellow soldiers ! for God's sake fire ! ' and instantly they gave the British a full volley.

" In a few minutes the British retreated, and the Americans took possession of the bridge.

" Their volley had killed three British soldiers, two of whom were left on the ground. The Americans afterward buried them, and we shall find their graves only a few feet from the monument."

But other passengers had entered the car, and the train was now in motion.

" There, that must do for the present," the Captain said; " the story will have to be finished after we leave the train."

Their first halt was at Lexington where they viewed with much interest the ground where the skirmish took place, the monument commemorating the devotion of those who fell, and everything to be found that had any connection with the events which have made the place famous in the annals of our country.

Evelyn Leland gazed long at the inscription on the monument, then read aloud, —

" Sacred to the Liberty and the Rights of Mankind!!! The Freedom and Independence of America — sealed and defended with the blood of her sons — This Monument is erected by the Inhabitants of Lexington . . . to the memory of their fellow citizens . . . the first victims of the sword of British Tyranny and Oppression, on the morning of the ever-memorable nineteenth of April, A. D. 1775. The Die was Cast!!! The blood of these Martyrs in the Cause of God and their Country was the Cement of the Union of these States, then Colonies, and gave the Spring to the Spirit, Firmness and Resolution of their Fellow citizens. They rose as one man to revenge their Brethren's blood and at the point of the sword to assert and defend their native Rights. They nobly dared to be

Free!!! The contest was long, bloody and affecting. Righteous Heaven approved the Solemn Appeal; Victory crowned their Arms, and the Peace, Liberty and Independence of the United States of America was their glorious Reward. Built in the year 1799.''

" You did n't read it all, Eva," said Walter; " you skipped the names."

" Yes," she said, " because I did n't want to take time to read it all; though I 'd be ever so unwilling to rob the poor, dear, brave fellows of any of the credit that belongs to them."

CHAPTER XII.

FROM Lexington our little party went on at once to Concord. There they saw the monument, and near it the graves of the two British soldiers of whom the Captain had spoken as having fallen in the fight.

" The British entered Concord in two divisions," he said ; " one by the main road, the other passing over the hill north of it. Captain Beeman, of Petersham, and other Tories had given them information in regard to the stores secreted in Concord, and Captain Parsons with six companies was sent to destroy them."

" Sent where, Papa ? " asked Lulu.

" To the house of Colonel Barrett," replied her father. " Captain Lawrie, with three companies was stationed at the North Bridge, just here. The monument stands upon the very spot where the British stood, and on yon plain across the river is where the American militia were when the fire of the British killed Hosmer and Davis.

" Colonel Smith, in the village, heard the firing, and sent a reinforcement to Lawrie's help ; but seeing that the militia were increasing in numbers, they turned about and joined in the retreat. Then the party under Captain Parsons, who, you will remember, had gone to Colonel Barrett's to destroy the secreted stores, returned, and were allowed by the militia to pass the bridge unmolested."

"Why did n't they attack them, Captain?" asked Eva, "were n't they strong enough?"

"Yes; but war had not yet been declared, and the colonists had been enjoined to act only on the defensive and let Great Britain be the aggressor.

"Besides, the militia at Concord had not yet heard of the slaughter of their brethren at Lexington. They themselves had just killed three British soldiers, to be sure, but it was purely in self-defence."

"The British started back to Boston pretty soon after that, did n't they, Papa?" asked Lulu.

"Yes; Colonel Smith thought it prudent, seeing how rapidly the militia were gathering, to return at once, and a little after twelve o'clock began his retreat toward Lexington, covering his main column by strong flanking guards.

"As you may suppose, the people had become intensely excited by this time, and I dare say very many were burning to avenge the slaughter of their comrades They no longer adhered to the cautious counsels given them at Concord, and secreting themselves behind barns and fences, fired upon the British troops as they passed. All along the line of march to Lexington the British were terribly galled in this way. Guns were fired with sure aim from every house, barn, and stone wall. As we noticed in coming here the road between this town and Lexington passes through a hilly country, as well calculated as possible for such work. At almost every wooded defile numbers of the British were picked off by concealed marksmen, and at Hardy's Hill there was a severe skirmish.

" There was no longer any military order among the Americans, but each man fought as he deemed best. Some of them were killed by the British flankers coming suddenly upon them in their places of concealment, but their numbers were comparatively small.

" Several of the British were shot near the battle-ground of the morning at Lexington, and Colonel Smith was badly wounded in the leg at Fiske's Hill, near the town."

" So they did n't have a very good time on their march back to Boston," remarked Max.

" No, very far from it," replied his father. " You will remember they had been marching the night before, marching and fighting pretty much all that day, and attacked every now and then by a concealed foe, who shot down one after another; they became at last so fatigued that they must have surrendered to the Americans if reinforcements had not reached them.

" I have said a request for help had been sent to General Gage from Lexington early in the morning, and he had responded with about nine hundred men under Lord Percy, — three regiments of infantry and two divisions of marines. These left Boston about nine o'clock in the morning and marched toward Lexington.

" As they passed through Roxbury they played ' Yankee Doodle' in derision, having before used it as a Rogue's March."

" Papa," Gracie asked, " did the Roxbury people know about the fight at Lexington and Concord?"

" They had heard vague rumours of a fight at Lexington, and the marching in that direction of these Boston troops confirmed their worst fears."

" What an excitement the marching of those British troops must have caused all along the way as they went !" exclaimed Eva.

" Yes," replied Captain Raymond, " one of their officers said, ' they [the Americans] seemed to drop from the clouds.'"

" Percy's brigade met them about half a mile from Lexington. He formed a hollow square, and for its defence, planted a cannon on high ground near Monroe's tavern, and received into his enclosure the wearied troops of Smith. Some of them were so heated and worn out that they lay exhausted and panting upon the ground, their tongues hanging out of their mouths, as a dog's does when he is tired and overheated.

" But Percy did not dare allow them to rest long, for the militia had gathered from all quarters, and the woods were swarming with minute-men. They were given a little refreshment, a brief rest, then hurried on their way, committing as they went deeds of ruffianism of which they had reason to be heartily ashamed ; property was destroyed, houses were plundered, and several innocent persons were murdered.

" Of course the Americans were filled with indignation as well as grief for the sufferings of friends and neighbours, some of them their near kindred."

" Yes ; oh, it was just dreadful, Papa ! " exclaimed Gracie, her eyes filling with tears. " I think the British of those days were very, very cruel."

" Very true," replied her father ; " there were very many deeds of blood and violence, for which there was no excuse, committed by them during that war. Rawdon, Tarleton, and even Cornwallis showed themselves men of savage cruelty."

" Yes," exclaimed Rosie, " I perfectly detest and abhor that brutal Tarleton ! No Indian was ever more heartless and cruel than he ! "

" I think that is true," the Captain said. " He treated American prisoners so unfortunate as to fall into his hands, with most inhuman cruelty; also he was so vain, conceited, and untruthful that in a ' History of the Campaigns of 1780 and 1781 in the Southern Provinces of North America,' which he wrote after his return to England, he distorts events for his self-glorification to such a degree as has seldom been paralleled. Yes, take him all together he was, I think, one of the most despicable characters of the Revolution."

" I have always been so glad over his defeat by Morgan at the battle of the Cowpens," said Eva, " and have always admired the reminders of it given him by some of the Southern ladies, particularly of the wound on his hand that Colonel Washington gave him in chasing him from that battle-field."

" Yes, I remember," said Rosie. " The ladies were great admirers of Colonel Washington, talked a great deal about him, and at least two or three times gave that vain, boastful, cruel Tarleton a rub about that wound."

" Yes," said the Captain, " those sallies of wit were expended on him by two sisters, — daughters of Colonel Montfort, of Halifax County, North Carolina. When Cornwallis was there on his way to Virginia, Colonel Washington was the subject of conversation one evening; and Tarle-

ton, nettled doubtless by the admiration freely
expressed by the ladies, began talking against
him, saying that he was an illiterate fellow,
hardly able to write his own name.

"The remark was made in the presence of
Mrs. Willie Jones, one of the sisters I have
spoken of, and she replied, 'Ah, Colonel, you
ought to know better, for you bear on your
person proof that he knows very well *how to
make his mark.*'"

"I should n't have liked to be in his place,"
remarked Max. "I dare say he felt like shoot-
ing Mrs. Jones for her compliment."

"That is not at all unlikely," said his father.
"It is said that when her sister, Mrs. Ashe,
twitted him in like manner, he showed his temper
plainly. He had been talking again, sarcasti-
cally of Colonel Washington, in her presence,
and finally said with a sneer, 'I would be happy
to see Colonel Washington.' To which she instantly replied, 'If you had looked behind you,
Colonel Tarleton, at the battle of the Cowpens,
you would have enjoyed that pleasure.'"

"That was just good for him!" exclaimed
Lulu. "I wonder what he said to it, — if he
answered her at all."

"He was very angry (for no doubt the words
stung him) and laid his hand on the hilt of his
sword, while he regarded her with a frown,"
replied the Captain. "But General Leslie, his

superior officer said, ' Say what you please, Mrs. Ashe; Colonel Tarleton knows better than to insult a lady in my presence.' "

" Did Tarleton ever insult a lady, Papa?" asked Gracie.

" I have read that he once insulted an American woman, — one who was large and strong, — and that she knocked him down upon the floor, seized him by the throat, and choked him till he was black in the face; she probably would have killed him if some one had not come to his assistance and pulled her off."

" Surely he must have been proud of *that* encounter," laughed Max.

CHAPTER XIII.

THERE were several more souvenirs of the Revolution shown the young people by Captain Raymond that morning, — among them Boston's " Liberty Tree," or rather the sculptured representation of it set within a niche on the front of a house, and exactly over the spot on which the tree stood before its destruction by the British during the siege of Boston.

" It was under that tree the association calling themselves 'Sons of Liberty' used to hold their meetings," he said. " They met there in the summer of 1765 when there was a great excitement over the passage of the Stamp Act by the British Parliament, and continued to do so until the destruction of the tree by the British during the siege of Boston, 1775. It was called 'Liberty Tree' and the ground under it 'Liberty Hall.'

"A newspaper of that time, the 'Essex Gazette,' of Aug. 31st, 1775, describes the destruction of the tree. It says, 'They made a furious attack upon it and after a long spell of laughing, grinning, sweating and foaming with malice diabolical they cut down the tree because it bore the

name of Liberty. A soldier was killed by falling
from one of its branches during the operation.'"

It was dinner time when our party reached the
hotel, where they had left Grandma Elsie and
Violet with the little ones and their maids. The
ladies had not cared to join in the morning's
excursion as they wanted to do a little shopping,
and had already seen Concord, Lexington, and
the places of historical interest in the city itself.

But Bunker Hill was to be visited that afternoon, and from that little trip neither lady asked
to be excused. They all went together, starting
directly after leaving the table.

Every one greatly enjoyed the view from the
top of the monument; it was like a vast paint-
ing, showing them the city of Boston with its
harbour, where could be seen vessels from almost
every part of the world, and the many towns
and villages in its vicinity, each with its own
story of its struggles for liberty in " the days that
tried men's souls." Far in the northwest the
higher peaks of New Hampshire's White Mountains were visible; on the northeast they could
discern the peninsula of Nahant, while still
farther in the distance was Cape Ann.

The Captain gave them a brief account of the
erection of the monument.

" It was not till 1824 that a movement was
made to that end," he said. " General La Fayette
was at the time the nation's guest, and was in-

vited to lay the corner-stone, which he did on the 17th of June, 1825, the fiftieth anniversary of the battle.

" The Hon. Daniel Webster made an oration on the subject to an immense crowd which had gathered for the occasion. There were forty of the survivors of the battle present, and probably La Fayette met more of his fellow-soldiers of that war then than at any other time or place."

" Was it finished in that year, Papa? " asked Lulu.

" No, indeed, my child; not for seventeen years. The last stone was raised about six o'clock on the morning of the 23d of July, 1842, and with it — waving the American Flag as he went up — was Mr. Edward Carnes, Jr., of Charlestown, the roar of cannon at the same time announcing the event to the surrounding country."

" But that was n't the anniversary of the battle ? " remarked Rosie, in a tone of inquiry.

" No," the Captain said; " but on the next anniversary, — June 17th, 1843, — the monument was dedicated. Daniel Webster was the orator on that occasion also, addressing a vast audience composed of citizens and soldiers."

" Oh, how I would have liked to hear his speech, if only he could have waited till I was in this world and old enough to understand what he was talking about ! " exclaimed Rosie.

A remark which called forth a good-humoured laugh from her hearers.

"Now, Papa, the next thing is to tell us about the battle of Bunker Hill, — is n't it?" Lulu said with a bright, coaxing look up into his face.

"I suppose so," he replied, with an indulgent smile. "But first let us look at these cannon, — the ' Hancock ' and the ' Adams ; ' you will readily understand for whom they were named. They belonged formerly to the Ancient and Honourable Artillery Company. This one — the ' Adams ' — you see is not sound ; it was burst in firing a salute. You also see that they bear an inscription, which I shall read aloud for the benefit of the company : —

" Sacred to Liberty. This is one of four cannons which constituted the whole train of field-artillery possessed by the British colonies of North America at the commencement of the war, on the nineteenth of April, 1775. This cannon and its fellow, belonging to a number of citizens of Boston, were used in many engagements during the war. The other two, the property of the government of Massachusetts, were taken by the enemy. By order of the United States in Congress assembled, May nineteenth, 1788."

"What strong faith in God and the righteousness of their cause they must have had, to begin a war with Great Britain with only four cannon in their possession!" remarked Grandma Elsie.

" Yes," responded the Captain; " and it was by His good help that they conquered in spite of the seemingly insurmountable obstacles in their way. It was a fearful struggle, but with God and the armies of heaven on their side they could not fail.

" The events of that ever-memorable 19th of April were speedily heralded over the whole land, from the scenes of their occurrence down to South Carolina and Georgia, west to the first settlers of Kentucky, and north to Montreal and Quebec.

" It electrified its hearers, and with one impulse they of the colonies — soon to become States — sprang to arms. As Bancroft says, ' With one spirit they pledged themselves to each other to be ready for the extreme event.' With one heart the .continent cried, ' Liberty or death ! '

" The Massachusetts Committee of Safety sent a circular to the several towns of that State, conjuring them to encourage enlistments by every means in their power, and send the troops forward to headquarters at Cambridge with the expedition that the urgency and importance of the affair demanded. But the people had not waited for the call.

" Hearing of the slaughter of their brethren, men snatched their firelocks from the walls and rushed to the camp, often with scarcely any pre-paration, some of them with almost no provision, no money in their pockets, and only the clothes on their backs. They were hastening to the defence of their country and their endangered brethren.

" So Boston was besieged ; Prescott of Pepperell and his Middlesex minute-men kept watch over the entrance to that city. Gage was forced to fortify the town at all points, while the Americans talked of driving him and his troops into the sea.

" New Hampshire sent men under the command of John Stark, a noble fellow well known as brave, fearless, and worthy of all confidence.

" Israel Putnam was another, who, hearing the cry from Lexington, which reached him on the morning after the battle, while he was helping his hired men to build a stone wall on his farm, hurried thither without waiting to so much as change the check shirt he was wearing in the field ; though first he roused the militia officers of the nearest towns.

" He reached Cambridge by sunrise the next morning, having ridden the same horse a hundred miles in eighteen hours. He was full of courage and love for his country, and hundreds had already chosen him for their leader.

" Benedict Arnold was still another who made haste to Boston to assist in the siege. By the 21st of April it was estimated that twenty thousand men were collected about that city.

" The battle of Bunker Hill, you will recollect, was not fought till the 17th of June. During all the intervening time the Americans had kept the British officers and their troops besieged in Boston, and they were beginning to be much ashamed of their confinement.

" The Americans had decided to throw up a breast-work across the road near Prospect Hill, and to fortify Bunker Hill as soon as a supply of powder and artillery could be obtained; but learning that Gage had planned to extend his lines north and south over Dorchester and Charlestown, and had fixed upon the eighteenth of June for so doing, they decided to anticipate his movement, and on the fifteenth of that month the Massachusetts Committee of Safety informed the Council of War that, in their opinion, Dorchester Heights should be fortified; and they recommended unanimously the establishing of a post on Bunker Hill.

" The choice of an officer to conduct the enterprise fell upon William Prescott, who was colonel of a regiment; and the next evening a brigade of a thousand men was put under his command.

" Soon after sunset they paraded on Cambridge Common. They were not in uniform as American troops would be in these days, nor had they such arms; for the most part they had fowling-pieces, — no bayonets to them, — and only a small supply of powder and bullets, which they carried in horns and pouches.

" Four days previously a proclamation had been issued threatening all persons in arms against their sovereign with death under martial law, by the cord as rebels and traitors. That menace these men were the first to defy; and he, Prescott, was resolved ' never to be taken alive.'

" Langdon, the president of Harvard College, prayed fervently with them. Then as it began to grow dark on that summer night, they marched silently and without noise across the narrow isthmus, taking with them their wagons with intrenching tools; and Prescott, calling around him his officers and Richard Gridley, an experienced engineer, consulted with them as to the spot on which they should erect their earthworks.

" Bunker Hill had been proposed by the committee, but Prescott had received orders to march to Breed's Hill, and obeyed them. It was nearer Boston, and he and his companions thought it better suited than the other for annoying the British in the town and the shipping in the harbour.

" So the engineer drew there, by the light of the stars, the lines of a redoubt nearly eight rods square. The bells of Boston had struck twelve before they began their work by turning the first sod, but every man of the thousand plied the pickaxe and spade in turn, and so rapidly that

the parapet soon assumed form and height
sufficient for defence, and Prescott said to
himself, 'We shall keep our ground if some
screen, however slight, can be completed before
discovery.'

"He set a watch to patrol the shore, and
twice went down to the margin of the water, on
which three British vessels lay at anchor, — the
'Lively' in the ferry between Boston and Charlestown, and a little to the eastward of her the
'Falcon,' sloop-of-war, and the 'Somerset,' a ship-
of-the-line, — and listening intently he could hear
the drowsy cry of the sentinels on their decks,
'All is well.'"

Captain Raymond paused and looked at his
watch.

"It is time we were going," he said. "I will
just point out to you all the localities made interesting by the events of that day, and finish my
story on board the 'Dolphin,' to which we are
just about to return. We may be in the way of
other visitors here, but there will be quite to
ourselves, and an annoyance to no one."

They went back to their hotel, where the
Captain left them for a little, saying he had some
purchases to make for use on the voyage, but
would return shortly to see them on board the
yacht.

He was not gone very long, and on his return
the entire party — with the exception of Donald

Keith who had bidden them farewell early that morning — returned with him to the "Dolphin," which presently sailed out of the harbour and pursued her way up along the New England coast.

CHAPTER XIV.

THE evening proved a rainy one and cool for the season; but the "Dolphin's" cabin was found an agreeable resort. All gathered there, and at once there was an urgent request from the young people that the interrupted story of the battle of Bunker Hill might be resumed.

"You know, Papa, we left off just where Prescott's men were digging and making a redoubt," said Lulu. "The night before the battle, was n't it?"

"Yes," he replied. "The British were greatly astonished when daylight revealed the work that had been going on during the hours of darkness; for it was done so quietly that their suspicions had not been aroused.

"No shout disturbed the night
   Before that fearful fight;
   There was no boasting high,
   No marshalling of men
   Who ne'er might meet again;
   No cup was filled and quaffed to victory!
   No plumes were there,
   No banners fair,
   No trumpets breathed around;
   Nor the drum's startling sound
   Broke on the midnight air."

" What nice verses, Papa!" said Gracie.
" Did you make them yourself?"

" No, daughter," he replied, " it was merely
a quotation from John Neal, one of our own
American poets.

" But to go on with my story. As soon as the
British discovered the redoubt our men had constructed on Breed's Hill, the captain of the 'Lively'
put springs on his cables and opened a fire upon
it without waiting for orders.

" The noise of the cannon aroused the sleeping
people of Boston, and by the time the sun was up
every eminence and roof in the city swarmed
with them, all gazing with astonished eyes upon
the strange apparition on Breed's Hill. The
' Lively's ' shots did no harm, and the Americans
went on as before with their work. They were
behind their intrenchments busied in strengthen-
ing them, and toiled on till pick and shovel had to
be laid aside for guns to defend them with.

" The firing presently ceased for a little, by
order of Admiral Graves, the British naval commander-in-chief, but was soon resumed by the
shipping, while a battery of six guns on Copp's
Hill in the city joined in with them.

" Early that morning the British general, Gage,
called a council of war, and it was decided to
drive the Americans out of their works, and that
the attack should be made in front.

" Boston was full of excitement, drums were

beating, dragoons galloping about the streets, regulars and royalists marching and counter-marching, artillery trains rumbling and church-bells ringing."

" Ah, how the hearts of wives and mothers, brothers and sisters, must have been torn at thought of the terrible struggle just at hand!" sighed Grandma Elsie, as the Captain paused for a moment in his narrative.

" Yes," he replied, "then and still more when from the roofs, steeples, and every sort of eleva-tion, they watched with streaming eyes the pro-gress of the fight after it had actually begun."

" Oh," exclaimed Gracie, " how glad and thankful I am that God let us live in these later days when there is no war in our dear country ! "

" Yes, dear child, we should thank God for peace," her father responded, softly smoothing her hair and pressing his lips to her cheek for an instant as she stood by his side, her head resting lovingly on his shoulder.

" The Americans worked faithfully on their intrenchments all the morning," he continued, " Prescott doing all he could to encourage them by his voice and example, even walking leisurely around upon the parapet in full view of the Brit-ish officers who were still in Boston.

" It is said that Gage was looking at the American works through a field-glass, and saw

Prescott, who was a tall man of commanding appearance, going his rounds, and that he inquired of Counsellor Willard, a brother-in-law of Prescott, who was standing near, who it was.

" ' That is Colonel Prescott,' was the reply.

" ' Will he fight?' asked Gage.

" ' Yes, sir,' answered Willard, ' he is an old soldier, and will fight as long as a drop of blood remains in his veins.'

" ' The works must be carried immediately,' was Gage's rejoinder, and he at once proceeded to give the order for the attack.

" He sent between two and three thousand picked men under the command of Generals Howe and Pigot. They crossed the water in twenty-eight barges, and landed at Morton's Point beyond the eastern foot of Breed's Hill, covered by the guns of the 'Falcon' and other vessels. There they waited for reinforcements, which were sent Howe about two o'clock.

" While the troops of Howe and Pigot were waiting, they dined ; but the poor Americans behind their intrenchments, at which they had been working all the morning as well as from twelve o'clock of the previous night, had little or nothing to eat or drink, and were suffering with hunger, thirst, and the extreme heat of the weather as well as fatigue, for the day was one of the hottest of the season.

" Besides, the reinforcements sent to their assistance were, so few and feeble that a dreadful suspicion arose in their minds that they were the victims of treachery.

"Still they could not doubt the patriotism of their principal officers; and before the battle began, the arrival of their beloved Dr. Warren and General Pomeroy entirely relieved their doubts.

"Dr. Warren was suffering from sickness and exhaustion; and Putnam, who was at Cambridge forwarding reinforcements and provisions to Charlestown, tried to persuade him not to take part in the coming fight. But his heart was in the cause, and he was not to be induced to give up doing all he could to help in the approaching struggle for freedom.

"He mounted a horse, sped across the neck, and just as Howe gave orders to advance, entered the redoubt amid the loud cheers of the men who so loved and trusted him."

"Such a lovely man, and ardent patriot as he was!" exclaimed Violet. "Oh, it makes my heart ache to think that he was killed in that battle."

"It was a very great loss to the American cause," responded her husband, taking a book from a table near at hand as he spoke. "This," he said, "is Bancroft's History, which I bought this afternoon that I might have his help in going over the story of the battle of Bunker Hill and

13

other interesting events of the Revolution. This is what he says of Joseph Warren: —

" In him were combined swiftness of thought and re-solve, courage, endurance, and manners which won universal love. He opposed the British government not from interested motives nor from resentment. Guileless and intrepid, he was in truth a patriot. As the moment for the appeal to arms approached, he watched with joy the revival of the generous spirit of New England's ancestors; and wherever the peril was greatest he was present animating not by words alone, but ever by his example.

" His integrity, the soundness of his judgment, his ability to write readily and well, his fervid eloquence, his exact acquaintance with American rights and the infringements of them, gave authority to his ad-vice in private and in the provincial congress. Had he lived, the future seemed burdened with his honors; he cheerfully sacrificed all for the freedom of his country and the rights of man."

"He left some children, if I remember right?" remarked Violet in a tone of inquiry, as her husband paused in his reading.

" Yes, four of them," answered the Captain; " and his wife having died about two years be-fore, they were now left orphans, in straitened circumstances.

" And that reminds me of a good deed done by Gen. Benedict Arnold. He was a warm friend of Warren, and for that reason came to their relief, himself contributing five hundred dollars for their education, and obtaining from Congress the amount of a major-general's half pay, to be applied to their support from the time of their father's death until the youngest child should be of age.

" But to go on with the account of the battle. Warren had been entreated not thus to expose his life. His answer was, ' It is sweet and becoming to die for one's country.' He saw all the difficulties in the way of his countrymen, and desired to give all the help in his power.

" Putnam expressed himself as ready to receive his orders ; but Warren declined to take the command from him, and passed on to the redoubt which seemed likely to be the chief point of attack by the enemy.

" Prescott there offered the command to him, as Putnam had just done ; but Warren again declined, saying, ' I come as a volunteer, to learn from a soldier of experience.' This though three days before he had been elected a provincial major-general.

" After the British had landed and before the battle began, Col. John Stark arrived with his New Hampshire troops. Except Prescott he brought the largest number into the field. He was a very brave man, and so cool and collected that he marched leisurely across the isthmus, raked by the cannon of the enemy ; and when one of his captains advised a quickstep, he replied, 'One fresh man in action is worth ten fatigued ones.'

" There was not time for him to consult with Prescott. They fought independently, — Prescott at his redoubt, Stark and Knowlton, and Reed's regiment to protect its flank.

" Months before that, — two days after the battle of Concord, — Gage had threatened to burn Charlestown in case the Americans should occupy the heights. So an order was now given to set it on fire, and it was done by shells from Copp's Hill; the houses being mostly of wood, two hundred of them were soon in flames.

" The British thought to be protected in their advance by the smoke of the burning houses, but a gentle breeze, the first that had been felt that day, arose and wafted it aside, so that they were not hidden from the eyes of the Americans.

" It was somewhere between two and three o'clock when the British began their approach. They were in two columns, one led by Howe, the other by Pigot, Howe no doubt expecting to get into Prescott's rear and force him to a surrender. But I will give another extract from Bancroft.

" As they began to march, the battery on Copp's Hill, from which Clinton and Burgoyne were watching every movement, kept up an incessant fire, which was seconded by the 'Falcon' and the 'Lively,' the 'Somerset' and the two floating batteries; the town of Charlestown, consisting of five hundred edifices of wood, burst into a blaze; and the steeple of its only church became a pyramid of fire. All the while the masts of the British shipping and the heights of the British camp, the church towers, the house tops of a populous town, and the acclivities of the surrounding country, were crowded with spectators to watch the battle which was to take place in full sight on a conspicuous eminence."

"Oh, Papa," pleaded Gracie, as he paused for an instant, "please tell it. I like that so much better than listening to reading."

"Quite a compliment to me as a reader," he returned with an amused look.

"No, sir, as a talker. I like to hear you tell things," she responded, with a sweet, engaging smile.

"Do you, dear child? Very well, I'll try to gratify you.

"When Prescott saw the red-coats moving toward his redoubt he ordered two separate detachments to flank the enemy, then went through his works encouraging his men, to whom this was an entirely new experience. 'The red-coats will never reach the redoubt,' he said, 'if you will but withhold your fire till I give the order; and be careful not to shoot over their heads.' Then he waited till the enemy had come within a few rods, when waving his sword over his head he gave the word, ' Fire ! '

" Every gun was instantly discharged, and nearly the whole of the front rank fell; the rest, astonished at this unexpected resistance, stood still. Then for some minutes the fire of the Americans continued, answered by the British, till at last they staggered, wavered, then fled down the hill toward their boats.

" Howe had been treated to a like reception by Stark's and Knowlton's troops, cheered on by Putnam who, like Prescott, bade them reserve their fire till the best moment, when they poured in one as deadly and destructive as that which came from Prescott's redoubt."

" Was n't Prescott's order to his men to reserve their fire till they could see the whites of the British soldier's eyes ? " queried Violet.

" Yes, so Lossing tells us ; and that he added, ' Then aim at their waistbands ; and be sure to pick off the commanders, known by their handsome coats.'

" His men were filled with joy when they saw the British fly, and wanted to pursue them, some even leaping the fence ; but their more prudent officers restrained them, and in a few minutes they were all within their works again, and ready to receive and repulse a second attack.

" Colonel Prescott praised and encouraged them while Putnam rode over to Bunker Hill to urge on reinforcement; but 'few additional troops could be brought to Breed's Hill before the second attack was made.' Before that the British were reinforced by four hundred marines from Boston, then they moved against the redoubt in the same order as at first, their artillery doing more damage to the Americans than in the first assault."

"Papa," asked Gracie, "what had become of the wounded men they'd left lying on the ground? — those the Americans shot down at their first fire over the redoubt?"

"They were still lying there on the ground where they had fallen, poor fellows! and the others marched over them. Ah, war is a dreadful thing, and those who forced it upon the patient, long-suffering Americans were either very thoughtless or exceeding cruel."

"Yes," exclaimed Rosie, "I don't know what George III. could have been made of to be willing to cause so much suffering even to innocent defenceless women and children, just that he might play the tyrant and forcibly take from the Americans their own hard earnings to pay his way."

"He was perhaps not quite so wicked as weak," replied her mother; "you know, I think, that he afterward lost his mind several times. Indeed he had done so once before this, — in 1764."

" He had been wicked and cruel enough for a guilty conscience to set him crazy, I should think," remarked Max.

" Please go on, again, Papa, won't you?" entreated Lulu.

" I will," he said. " The British fired as they drew near, but with little effect; and the Americans, reserving their fire as before, till the foe was within five or six yards of the redoubt, then poured it on them with deadly aim, as at the first attack. It told with terrible effect; whole ranks of officers and men fell dead."

" Oh, did n't they run then, Papa?" queried Gracie with a shudder of horror as she seemed to see the ground strewed with the dead and dying.

" They were thrown into confusion and retreated to the shore," the Captain replied, — " retreated in great disorder. It seemed that the American fire was even more fatal than before. In telling the story afterward Prescott said, ' From the whole American line there was a continuous stream of fire.'

" The British officers exposed themselves fearlessly, and urged their soldiers on with persuasions, threats, and even blows; but they could not reach the redoubt, and presently gave way, and, as I have said, retreated in great disorder.

" At one time Howe was left nearly alone for a few seconds, so many of his officers had been killed or wounded; while 'the dead,' as Stark said in his account of the battle, 'lay as thick as sheep in a fold.'

"Now I think my little Gracie will have to put up with some more reading," added the Captain, with a smiling glance at her; then opening his book, read aloud, —

"At intervals the artillery from the ships and batteries was playing, while the flames were rising over the town of Charlestown and laying waste the places of the graves of its fathers, and streets were falling together, and ships at the yards were crashing on the stocks, and the kindred of the Americans, from the fields, and hills and house-tops around, watched every gallant act of their defenders. 'The whole,' wrote Burgoyne, 'was a complication of horror and importance beyond anything it ever came to my lot to be witness to. It was a sight for a young soldier that the longest service may not furnish again.'"

"If," remarked Captain Raymond, again closing the book, "it was so dreadful a sight for soldiers accustomed to the horrors of war, what must it not have been to the American farmers taking their first lesson in war? But not one of them shrank from duty. I think we may be very proud of those countrymen of ours. Prescott said to his men, 'If we drive them back once more they cannot rally again.' At that his men cheered him, and shouted, 'We are ready for the red-coats again.'

" But alas ! the officers now discovered that the supply of gunpowder was nearly exhausted. Prescott had sent in the morning for more, but it had not come ; and there were not fifty bayonets in his party."

" They were wonderfully brave to stand for a third attack under such circumstances," remarked Evelyn.

" They were indeed," responded the Captain. " No one of the seven hundred men with Prescott seems to have thought of giving up the contest without another effort. Some gathered stones from the redoubt to use as missiles, those who had no bayonets resolved to club their guns and strike with them when their powder should be gone ; all were determined to fight as long as a ray of hope of success could be discerned. And they did.

" They waited with quiet firmness the approach of the enemy who came steadily on with fixed bayonets, while their cannon were so trained that they swept the interior of the breast-work from one end to the other, obliging the Americans to crowd within their fort.

" The Americans were presently attacked on three sides, at once ; and there were, as I have said, but seven hundred of them, some of whom had no more than one round of ammunition, none of them more than four. But they did not quail, and Prescott calmly gave his directions.

" He bade his men wait, reserving their fire till the enemy was within twenty yards. Then they poured in a deadly volley. Every shot told. Howe was wounded in the foot, and several of his officers were killed besides the common soldiers. But they pressed on to the now nearly silent redoubt, for the American fire had slackened and begun to die away.

" And now there was only a ridge of earth between the combatants, and the first of the British who reached it were assailed with a shower of stones. Then some of them scaled the parapet and were shot down in the act. One of these was Major Pitcairn, who had led the troops at Lexington. As he mounted the parapet he cried out, ' Now for the glory of the marines ! ' and was answered by a shot from a negro that gave him a mortal wound. His son carried him to a boat, conveyed him to Boston, and there he soon died."

" Oh ! " exclaimed Gracie, " I hope that brave Colonel Prescott did n't get killed, Papa ! "

" No : he escaped unhurt, though his coat and waistcoat were pierced and torn in several places by the bayonets of the British, which he parried with his sword.

" It was now a hand-to-hand fight, British and Americans mingled together, our men walking backward and hewing their way out, dealing deadly blows with their muskets.

" Fortunately the British were too much exhausted to use their bayonets with vigour ; and so intermingled were they and the Americans that the use of firearms would have been dangerous to their own men as well as to ours."

"Oh," sighed Rosie, "I have always been so sorry that our men did n't have plenty of gunpowder! I don't think there 's a doubt that if they had been well supplied with it, they would have won a grand victory."

"Yes ; they did wonders considering all they had to contend with," said the Captain. "Their courage, endurance, and skill as marksmen astonished the British, and were never forgotten by them during the long war that followed.

"The number engaged in the battle of Bunker Hill was small, all taken together not more than fifteen hundred of the Americans, — less than seven hundred in the redoubt, — while of the British there were, according to Gage, more than two thousand ; other and accurate observers said, ' near upon three thousand.'

"But in spite of the smallness of the numbers engaged, the battle was one of the severest and most determined on record. Neither side could claim a victory, but both displayed great courage and determination."

"And Joseph Warren was one of the killed ! " sighed Grandma Elsie , " one of the bravest, best, and most lovable of men, as those who knew him have testified. I remember reading that Mrs.

John Adams said of him and his death, ' Not all the havoc and devastation they have made has wounded me like the death of Warren. We want him in the Senate ; we want him in his profession ; we want him in the field. We mourn for the citizen, the senator, the physician, and the warrior.' General Howe said, ' His death was worth more to the British than that of five hundred of the provincial privates.' "

" And that was not an over-estimate, I think," said the Captain. " It was indeed a sad loss to the cause of the colonies when he was slain."

" But there were more of the British killed than of our men, — were n't there, Papa ? " asked Lulu.

" Yes, very many more. By Gage's own account the number of killed and wounded in his army was at least one thousand and fifty-four. The oldest soldiers had never seen anything like it, — so many officers killed and wounded. Bancroft tells us that the battle of Quebec, which won a continent, did not cost the lives of so many officers as the battle of Bunker Hill, which gained nothing ' but a place of encampment.'

" The American loss was one hundred and forty-five in killed and missing, three hundred and four wounded. No doubt the loss would have been very much greater but for the brave conduct of the men at the rail fence and the bank of the Mystic, who kept the enemy at bay while the men from the redoubt retreated. You may remember that they were Stark's men from New Hampshire and Knowlton's from Connecticut."

"I hope the result of the battle encouraged the Americans as much as it discouraged the British," remarked Rosie, "and I think I have read that it did."

"Yes," the Captain replied, "it did. In his general order, thanking the officers and soldiers for their gallant behaviour at Charlestown, Ward said, 'We shall finally come off victorious, and triumph over the enemies of freedom and America.'"

"Did they fight any more that night, Papa?" asked Gracie.

"No," he said, "though Prescott went to headquarters and offered to recover his post if he might have three fresh regiments. He did not seem to think he had done anything more than his duty, and asked for neither praise nor promotion, though others gave him unstinted praise for what he had done.

"Putnam was absent from the field, engaged in trying to collect reinforcements, when the third attack was made, and the retreating party encountered him on the northern declivity of Bunker Hill. He tried to stop and turn them about, — commanded, pleaded, and used every exertion in his power to rally the scattered corps, swearing that victory should crown the American arms. ' Make a stand here ; we can stop them yet ! ' he exclaimed. ' In God's name, fire, and give them one shot more ! '

" It is said that after the war was over he made a sincere confession to the church of which he was a member; but he said, ' It was almost enough to make an angel swear to see the cowards refuse to secure a victory so nearly won.' "

" And could n't he stop them, Papa ? " asked Gracie.

" He succeeded with some few," replied her father, " joined them to a detachment which had not reached the spot till the fighting was over, and with them took possession of Prospect Hill, where he encamped for the night."

" Oh, Papa, what did they do with all those Americans and British who had been killed ? " asked Gracie.

" There must have been many a sad funeral," the Captain said in reply, " many a widow and fatherless child to weep over the slain. Ah, let us thank our heavenly Father for the liberty and security bought for us at so fearful a price."

" Yes," responded Grandma Elsie ; " and let us keep them for ourselves and our children by ' the eternal vigilance which is the price of liberty.' "

CHAPTER XV.

To the great delight of the young people on board the " Dolphin " the sun shone in a clear sky the next morning.

Soon after breakfast they were all on deck, as usual in pleasant weather, enjoying the breeze, the sight of passing vessels, and a distant view of the land.

The Captain and Violet sat near together with the two little ones playing about them, while Grandma Elsie, in a reclining chair, at no great distance, seemed absorbed in a book.

" Mamma is reading something sad, I know by the look on her face," said Walter, hurrying toward her, the others following. " What is it you are reading, Mamma, that makes you look so sorry? " he asked, putting an arm about her neck, and giving her a kiss. " Oh, that 's Bancroft's History ! "

" Yes," she said, " I was just looking over his account of the battles of Lexington and Concord, and some things he tells do make me sad though they happened more than a hundred years ago."

" Oh, please read them to us ! " pleaded sev-eral young voices, all speaking at once.

" I will give you some passages," she said; "not the whole, because you have already been over that ground. It is what he tells of Isaac Davis that particularly interests me," and she began reading.

" At daybreak the minute-men of Acton crowded, at the drum-beat, to the house of Isaac Davis, their captain, who ' made haste to be ready.' Just thirty years old, the father of four little ones, stately in his person, a man of few words, earnest even to solemnity, he parted from his wife, saying, ' Take good care of the children; ' and while she gazed after him with resignation, he led off his company.

" Between nine and ten the number of Americans on the rising ground above Concord Bridge had increased to more than four hundred. Of these there were twenty-five minute-men from Bedford, with Jonathan Wilson for their captain; others were from Westford, among them Thaxter, a preacher; others from Lit-tleton, from Carlisle, and from Chelmsford. The Acton company came last and formed on the right. The whole was a gathering not so much of officers and soldiers as of brothers and equals, of whom every one was a man well known in his village, observed in the meeting-house on Sundays, familiar at town meetings and respected as a freeholder or a freeholder's son. . . . ' The Americans had as yet received only uncertain rumors of the morning's events at Lexington. At the sight of fire in the village, the impulse seized them to march into the town for its defence.' But were they

not subjects of the British king ?   Had not the troops
come out in obedience to acknowledged authorities ?
Was resistance practicable?   Was it justifiable ?   By
whom could it be authorized?   No union had been
formed, no independence proclaimed, no war declared.
The husbandmen and mechanics who then stood on the
hillock by Concord river were called on to act, and
their action would be war or peace, submission or independence. Had they doubted they must have despaired.
Prudent statesmanship would have asked for time to
ponder.   Wise philosophy would have lost from hesitation the glory of opening a new era on mankind.   The
train-bands at Concord acted and God was with them.

" The American revolution grew out of the soul of
the people, and was an inevitable result of a living affection for freedom, which set in motion harmonious
effort as certainly as the beating of the heart sends
warmth and color through the system.   The rustic
heroes of that hour obeyed the simplest, the highest,
and the surest instincts, of which the seminal principle
existed in all their countrymen.   From necessity they
were impelled toward independence and self-direction ;
this day revealed the plastic will which was to attract
the elements of a nation to a centre, and by an innate
force to shape its constitution.

" The officers, meeting in front of their men, spoke
a few words with one another, and went back to their
places.   Barrett, the colonel, on horseback in the rear,
then gave the order to advance, but not to fire unless
attacked.   The calm features of Isaac Davis, of Acton,
became changed; the town school-master of Concord,
who was present, could never afterward find words
strong enough to express how deeply his face reddened

at the word of command. 'I have not a man that is afraid to go,' said Davis, looking at the men of Acton, and drawing his sword, he cried, ' March!' His company, being on the right, led the way toward the bridge, he himself at their head, and by his side Major John Buttrick, of Concord, with John Robinson, of Westford, lieutenant-colonel in Prescott's regiment, but on this day a volunteer, without command.

" These three men walked together in front, followed by minute-men and militia, in double file, trailing arms. They went down the hillock, entered the byroad, came to its angle with the main road, and there turned into the causeway that led straight to the bridge. The British began to take up the planks ; to prevent it, the Americans quickened their step. At this the British fired one or two shots up the river; then another, by which Luther Blanchard and Jonas Brown were wounded. A volley followed, and Isaac Davis and Abner Hosmer fell dead. Three hours before, Davis had bid his wife farewell. That afternoon he was carried home and laid in her bedroom. His countenance was pleasant in death. The bodies of two others of his company, who were slain that day, were brought to her house, and the three were followed to the village graveyard by a concourse of the neighbors from miles around. Heaven gave her length of days in the land which his self-devotion assisted to redeem. She lived to see her country reach the Gulf of Mexico and the Pacific; when it was grown great in numbers, wealth, and power, the United States in Congress bethought themselves to pay honors to her husband's martyrdom, and comfort her under the double burden of sorrow and of more than ninety years."

"Ninety years!" exclaimed Walter. "Oh what an old, *old* woman she was! I think they ought to have given it to her a great deal sooner, — don't you, Mamma?"

"I do, indeed," she replied. "What a dreadful time it was! The British soldiery behaved like savages or demons, — burning houses, murdering innocent unarmed people. One poor woman — a Mrs. Adams, ill in bed, with a baby only a week old — was driven out of her bed, out of her house, and had to crawl almost naked to a corn-shed with her little one in her arms, while the soldiers set fire to her house.

"They shot and killed an idiot perched on a fence looking at them as they passed; and they brutally murdered two aged, helpless, unarmed old men, stabbing them, breaking their skulls and dashing out their brains."

"I don't wonder the Americans shot down as many of them as they could!" exclaimed Max, in tones of hot indignation. "Men that did such things were not brave soldiers, but worse savages than the Indians. Oh, how I wish our people had had the abundance of good weapons and powder and balls that we have now! Then they'd have taught the insolent British a good lesson; they would soon have driven Gage and all his savage soldiery into the sea."

"I presume they would," said Mrs. Travilla; "but poor fellows! they were very destitute of such needed supplies. This is what Bancroft says about it : —

" All the following night, the men of Massachusetts streamed in from scores of miles around, old men as well as young. They had scarce a semblance of artillery or warlike stores, no powder, nor organization, nor provisions; but there they were, thousands with brave hearts, determined to rescue the liberties of their country.

" The night preceding the outrages at Lexington there were not fifty people in the whole colony that ever expected any blood would be shed in the contest; the night after, the king's governor and the king's army found themselves closely beleaguered in Boston."

" Did the news fly very fast all over the country, Mamma? " asked Walter.

" Very fast for those times," she replied; " you must remember that then they had neither railroads nor telegraph, but as Bancroft says, ' Heralds by swift relays transmitted the war messages from hand to hand, till village repeated it to village; the sea to the backwoods; the plains to the highlands; and it was never suffered to droop till it had been borne north and south, east and west, throughout the land.' "

" But there was n't any more fighting till the battle of Bunker Hill, was there, Mamma? " asked Walter.

" Yes," she replied, " there was the taking of

Ticonderoga and Crown Point early in May, by a party under the command of Ethan Allen; there were about a hundred 'Green Mountain Boys' and nearly fifty soldiers from Massachusetts besides the men of Connecticut. The thing was planned in Connecticut, and the expense borne there.

" Allen marched in the night to the shore of the lake opposite to Ticonderoga. A farmer named Beman offered his son Nathan as a guide, saying that he (the lad) had been used to playing about the fort with the boys of the garrison, and knew of every secret way leading into it.

" Allen accepted the offer, but there was a difficulty about getting boats in which to cross the lake. They had but few and day began to dawn. If the garrison should be aroused their expedition was likely to fail, for a great deal depended upon taking them by surprise; so Allen decided not to wait for the rear division to cross, but to make the attempt with the officers and eighty-three men who were already on that side. He drew up his men in three ranks on the shore and made them a little speech in a low tone: 'Friends and fellow-soldiers, we must this morning quit our pretensions to valour, or possess ourselves of this fortress; and inasmuch as it is a desperate attempt, I do not urge it on, contrary to will. You that will undertake voluntarily, poise your firelock '

" Instantly every firelock was poised. ' Face to the right ! ' he cried, putting himself at their head, Benedict Arnold close at his side, and they marched quietly and steadily up to the gate.

" The sentinel there snapped his fusee at Allen, but it missed fire, and he retreated within the fort. The Americans rushed in after him, another sentinel made a thrust at one of them, but they ran upon the guard, raising the Indian war-whoop, Allen giving the sentinel a blow upon the head with his sword that made him beg for quarter.

" Of course the shout of our men had roused the garrison ; and they sprang from their beds, and came rushing out only to be made prisoners.

" Then young Beman guided Allen to the door of the sleeping apartment of Delaplace, the commander. The loud shout of the Americans had waked him and his wife, and both sprang to the door as Allen gave three loud raps upon it with his sword and thundered out an order for the commander to appear if he would n't have his whole garrison sacrificed.

" Delaplace threw open the door, showing himself only half dressed, in shirt and drawers, with his pretty wife standing behind him peering over his shoulder. He immediately recognized Allen, for they were old friends, and assuming an air of authority, demanded his errand.

"Allen pointed to his men and said sternly, 'I order you instantly to surrender.'

"'By what authority do you demand it?' asked Delaplace.

"'In the name of the Great Jehovah and the Continental Congress,' thundered Allen, and raising his sword over his prisoner's head, commanded him to be silent and surrender immediately.

"Delaplace saw that it was useless to refuse, so surrendered, ordered his men to parade without arms, and gave them up as prisoners. There were forty-eight of them; and they, with the women and children, were sent to Hartford as prisoners of war."

"And what did our men get besides the soldiers and women and children, Mamma?" asked Walter.

"Cannon, and guns of various kinds, other munitions of war, a quantity of provisions and material for boat building, and so forth, besides the fortress itself, which Bancroft says had ' cost the British nation eight millions sterling, a succession of campaigns, and many lives, yet was won in ten minutes by a few undisciplined volunteers, without the loss of life or limb.'"

"Oh, that was the very best of it, I think," said Gracie. "War wouldn't be so very, very dreadful if it was all like that, — would it, Grandma Elsie?"

" No dear," Mrs. Travilla replied, smiling lovingly upon the little girl, and softly smoothing her golden curls.

" Was there any other fighting before the battle of Bunker Hill, Mamma?" queried Walter.

" Yes," she said, " there were some encounters along this New England coast."

" And Crown Point was taken too, — was n't it, Mamma?" asked Rosie.

" Ah, yes! I had forgotten that part of my story," replied her mother. " It was taken two days later than Ticonderoga, also without any bloodshed. About the same time that Ticonderoga was taken, there was a British ship called the ' Canceaux ' in the harbour of Portland. The captain's name was Mowat. On the 11th of May he and two of his officers were on shore, when a party of sixty men from Georgetown seized them.

" The officer who had been left in command of the vessel threatened what he would do if they were not released, and even began to bombard the town. Mowat was released at a late hour, but felt angry and revengeful, and succeeded in rousing the same sort of feeling in the admiral of the station.

" A month later the people of a town called Machias seized the captain of two sloops that had come into their harbour to be freighted with lumber, and convoyed by a king's cutter called the ' Margaretta.' The lumber was for the British

army at Boston, and they, the Americans, got
possession of the sloops, after taking the captain,
whom they seized in the ' meeting-house.' The
' Margaretta' did n't fire on the town, but slipped
away down the harbour in the dark that night,
and the next morning sailed out to sea.

" Then forty men, under the command of Capt.
Jeremiah O'Brien, pursued her in one of the captured sloops, and as she was a dull sailer, soon
overtook her. An obstinate sea-fight followed ;
the captain of the cutter was mortally wounded,
six of his men not so badly, and after an hour's
fight the ' Margaretta's ' flag was struck. It was
the first time the British flag was struck on the
ocean to Americans."

" But not the last by any means ! " cried Max,
exultantly ; " whatever may be said of our land
forces, America has always shown herself superior to Great Britain on the sea. I 'm very proud
of the fact that though at the beginning of the
last war with England we had but twenty vessels
(exclusive of one hundred and twenty gun-boats),
while England had ten hundred and sixty, we
whipped her."

" Quite true, Max," Mrs. Travilla said, smiling at the boy's ardent patriotism, " and I am as
proud of the achievements of our navy as you
can be ; but let us give all the glory to God
who helped the oppressed in their hard struggle
against their unjust and cruel oppressor."

"Yes, ma'am, I know," he answered; "America was most shamefully oppressed, and it was only by God's help that she succeeded in putting a stop to the dreadful treatment of her poor sailors. Just to think of the insolent way the British naval officers used to have of boarding our vessels and carrying off American-born men, who loved their own country and wanted to serve her, and forcing them even to serve against her, fairly makes my blood boil!" Max had in his excitement unconsciously raised his voice so that his words reached his father's ear.

The captain looked smilingly at Violet, "My boy is an ardent patriot," he said in a pleased tone. "Should we ever have another war (which Heaven forbid!), I hope he will do his country good service."

"I am sure he will if he lives to see that day," returned Violet; "but I agree with you in hoping the need of such service will never arise."

"But let us always remember," Evelyn said in reply to Max, "that those cruel, unjust deeds. and the feelings that prompted them, were not those of the English people, but of their Government and the aristocracy, — I suppose because of their hatred of republicanism, their desire to keep the masses of the people down, and themselves rich and powerful."

"Yes," said Rosie, "it was just pure pride and selfishness. They did n't like the doctrine of our Declaration of Independence that 'all men are created equal.'"

Mrs. Travilla was turning over the leaves of her book again.

"Mamma," said Walter, "have n't you something more to read to us?"

"Yes," she replied, and began at once.

"On the ninth (of June) the 'Falcon,' a British sloop of war, was seen from Cape Ann in chase of two schooners bound to Salem. One of these was taken; a fair wind wafted the other into Gloucester harbor. Linzee, the captain of the 'Falcon,' followed with his prize, and, after anchoring, sent his lieutenant and thirty-six men in a whale-boat and two barges to bring under his bow the schooner that had escaped.

"As the barge men boarded her at her cabin windows, men from the shore fired on them, killing three and wounding the lieutenant in the thigh. Linzee sent his prize and a cutter to cannonade the town. They did little injury; while the Gloucester men, with the loss of but two, took both schooners, the barges, and every man in them, Linzee losing half his crew."

"How vexed he must have been!" laughed Lulu. "Did he ever go back to take revenge, Grandma Elsie?"

"No, I think not," she said, "though Gage and the British admiral planned to do so, and also to wreak vengeance on the people of Portland, — then called Falmouth, — where, as you probably remember, Mowat had been held prisoner for a few hours in May of that same year.

"On the morning of the 16th of October Mowat again appeared in their harbour in command of a ship of sixteen guns, attended by three other vessels, and at half-past nine in the morning began firing upon the town.

"In five minutes several houses were in a blaze; then a party of marines landed and spread the conflagration. He burned down about three fourths of the town, — a hundred and thirty dwelling-houses, the public buildings, and a church, — and shattered the rest of the houses with balls and shells. The English account makes the destruction still greater. So far north winter begins early, and it was just at the beginning of a severe one that he thus turned the poor people of that town out of house and home into the cold, in poverty and misery."

"That was a Christian deed worthy of a Christian king," remarked Rosie, scornfully.

"Bancroft says," continued her mother, "that the indignation of Washington was kindled by 'these savage cruelties, this new exertion of despotic barbarity.' General Green said, 'Death and destruction mark the footsteps of the enemy; fight or be slaves is the American motto.'"

"And who wouldn't rather fight and die

fighting, than be a slave?" cried Max, his eyes
flashing. "Grandma Elsie," he said, "you
have n't told us a word about the American navy.
Did n't they begin one about that time?"

"I think they did, Max," was her reply;
"but suppose we call upon your father to tell
us about it. He is doubtless better informed
than I in everything relating to that branch of
the service."

"Papa, will you?" asked the lad, turning
toward the Captain and raising his voice a little.

"Will I do what, my son?"

"Tell us about the doings of the navy in
Revolutionary times, sir," replied Max, "as
Grandma Elsie has been telling of the fights
on land."

"Oh, do, Papa; won't you?" pleaded Lulu,
hastening to his side, the other girls and Walter
following, while Max gallantly offered to move
Grandma Elsie's chair nearer to his father and
Violet, which she allowed him to do, thanking
him with one of her rarely sweet smiles.

CHAPTER XVI.

THE Captain, gently putting aside the two little ones who were hanging lovingly about him, saw every one seated comfortably, and near enough to hear all he might say, then resuming his own seat, began the account they had asked for of the early doings of the embryo navy of their common country.

" We had no navy at all when the Revolutionary War began," he said. " Rhode Island, the smallest State in the Union, was the first of the colonies to move in the matter of building and equipping a Continental fleet. On October 3, 1775, its delegates laid before Congress the instructions they had received to do what they could to have that work begun.

" They met with great opposition there ; but John Adams was very strongly in its favour, and did for it all in his power.

" On the 5th of October, Washington was authorized to employ two armed vessels to intercept British store-ships, bound for Quebec ; on the 13th, two armed vessels, of ten and of fourteen guns, were voted ; and seventeen days

later, two others of thirty-six guns. That was
the beginning of our navy; and it was very
necessary we should have one to protect our
seaport towns and destroy the English ships sent
against us, also to make it more difficult and
hazardous for them to bring over new levies of
troops to deprive us of our liberties, and from
using their vessels to destroy our merchantmen,
and so put an end to our commerce.

"Rhode Island had bold and skilful seamen,
some of whom had had something to do with
British ships before the war began, — even as
early as 1772.

"In that year there was a British armed
schooner called the 'Gaspee,' in Narragansett Bay,
sent there to enforce obnoxious British laws.

"Its officers behaved in so tyrannical a manner
toward the Americans of the neighbourhood that
at length they felt it quite unbearable; and one
dark, stormy night in June, Capt. Abraham
Whipple, a veteran sailor, with some brother
seamen, went down the bay in open whale-boats,
set the 'Gaspee' on fire, and burned her.

"The British Government of course wanted to
punish them, but all engaged in the work of
destruction were so true to each other that it
was impossible to find out who they were; but
three years later — in 1775, the year that the war
began — the bay was blockaded by an English
frigate, and in some way her commander learned

that Whipple had been the leader of the men who destroyed the ' Gaspee.' He then wrote him a note."

" You, Abraham Whipple, on the seventeenth of June 1772, burnt his Majesty's vessel the ' Gaspee,' and I will hang you to the yard-arm."

" Whipple replied with a note."

To Sir James Wallace :

Sir, — Always catch a man before you hang him.

ABRAHAM WHIPPLE.

" Good ! " laughed Max ; " and I think he never did catch him, — did he, Papa ? "

" No, though he made every effort to do so, being greatly angered by the impudent reply."

" But you don't blame Whipple for answering him in that way, — do you, Papa ? " queried Lulu.

" I can't say that I do," her father said with a slight smile. " And I think the legislature of Rhode Island did a right and wise thing in fitting out two armed vessels to drive Sir James and his frigate out of Narragansett Bay, giving the command of them, and thus the honour of firing the first gun in the naval service of the Revolution, to Captain Whipple."

" Oh, that was splendid ! " cried several young voices.

" That gave Washington a hint," continued

15

the Captain, "and he authorized the fitting out of several vessels as privateers, manning them with these sailor-soldiers."

"What is a privateer, Papa?" asked Gracie.

"A vessel belonging to some private person, or to more than one, sailing in time of war, with a license from Government to seize, plunder, and destroy the vessels of the enemy, and any goods they may carry, wherever found afloat."

"And how do they differ from transports, brother Levis?" asked Rosie.

"Transports are vessels used for the carrying of troops, stores, and materials of war," he answered.

"Did they do their work well, Captain?" asked Evelyn.

"Some did, and some did not," he answered. "The most successful was Capt. John Manly, who had been thirty years, or nearly that, on the sea. He was a skilful fisherman of Marblehead, and Washington commissioned him as captain.

"He was doubtless well acquainted with the qualifications of the sailors of that part of the coast, and knew how to select a choice crew , at all events he was very successful in annoying the enemy, and soon had captured three ships as they entered Boston Harbour. One of them was laden with just such things as were badly needed by the Americans, then besieging Boston, — heavy guns, mortars, and intrenching tools.

" Manly became a terror to the British, and they tried hard to catch him."

" If they had, I suppose they 'd have hung him," remarked Lulu, half inquiringly.

" No doubt they would have been glad to do so," her father replied. " They sent out an armed schooner from Halifax to take him ; but he was too wary and skilful a commander to be easily caught, and he went on roaming along the seacoast of New England, taking prize after prize from among the British ships."

" What was the name of his vessel, Papa? " asked Max.

" The ' Lee.' It was not long before Congress created a navy, and Manly was appointed a captain in it. He did gallant service until he was taken prisoner by Sir George Collier in the ' Rainbow.' "

" Did they hang him, Papa?" asked Gracie, with a look of distress.

" No ; he was kept a prisoner, first on that vessel, then in Mill prison, Halifax, exchanged after a while, then again taken prisoner while in command of the ' Pomona,' held a prisoner at Barbadoes, but made his escape and took command of the privateer ' Jason.' He was afterward attacked by two privateers, ran in between them, giving both a broadside at once and making them strike their colours.

" Later he was chased by a British seventy-four, and to escape capture ran his ship aground on a sand-bar; afterward he succeeded in getting her off, fired thirteen guns as a defiance, and made his escape."

" Please tell us some more, brother Levis," urged Walter, as the Captain paused in his narrative; " we'd be glad to hear all the doings of our navy."

" That would make a long story indeed, my boy," the Captain said with a smile; " longer than could be told in one day or two. I will try to relate some few more occurrences of particular interest; and I advise you all to consult history on the subject after we get home. The coming winter will be a good time for that.

" In October, 1775, as I have already said, Congress resolved that a swift sailing-vessel, to carry ten carriage-guns and an appropriate number of swivels, should be fitted out for a cruise of three months for the purpose of intercepting British transports. They also formed a Marine Committee consisting of seven members, and ordered another vessel to be built, — the Marine Committee performing the duties now falling to the share of our Secretary of the Navy.

Later in that same year Congress ordered thirteen more vessels to be built. They were the ' Washington,' ' Randolph,' ' Warren,' ' Hancock,' ' Raleigh,' each carrying thirty-two guns; the ' Effingham,' ' Delaware,' ' Boston,' ' Virginia,' ' Providence,' ' Montgomery,' ' Congress ' and ' Trumble ; ' some of these were armed with twenty-eight, others with twenty-four guns."

" They made Abraham Whipple captain of one, — did n't they, Papa?" asked Max.

" Yes ; Nicholas Biddle, Dudly Saltonstall and John B. Hopkins captains of the others, and Esek Hopkins commander-in-chief. He was considered as holding about the same rank in the navy that Washington did in the army, and was styled indifferently admiral or commodore.

"Among the first lieutenants appointed was John Paul Jones, who became a famous commander before the war was over, — a great naval hero. But you have all heard of him I think."

" Oh, yes," said Rosie. " It was he who commanded the ' Bonhomme Richard ' in that hard-fought battle with the British ship ' Serapis.' "

" Yes," replied the Captain. " It was one of the most desperate conflicts on record, and resulted in victory for Jones and the ' Bonhomme Richard,' though she was so badly damaged, — ' counters and quarters driven in, all her lower-deck guns dismounted, on fire in two places, and six or seven feet of water in the hold ' — that she had to be abandoned, and sank the next morning.

" Pearson the captain of the ' Serapis,' though

defeated, had made so gallant a fight that he was knighted by the king. When Jones heard of it he said, ' He deserves it; and if I fall in with him again I'll make a lord of him.'

" I think he — Pearson — was more gallant than polite or generous; for on offering his sword to Jones after his surrender he said, ' I cannot, sir, but feel much mortification at the idea of surrendering my sword to a man who has fought me with a rope round his neck.' "

" Just like an Englishman! " exclaimed Max, hotly; " but what did Jones say in reply, Papa? "

" He returned the sword, saying, ' You have fought gallantly, sir, and I hope your king will give you a better ship. ' "

" That was a gentlemanly reply," said Lulu, " and I hope Jones got the credit he deserved for his splendid victory."

" Europe and America rang with his praises," said her father. " The Empress of Russia gave him the ribbon of St. Ann, the King of Denmark a pension, and the King of France a gold-mounted sword with the words engraved upon its blade, ' Louis XVI., rewarder of the valiant assertor of the freedom of the sea.' He also made him a Knight of the Order of Merit.

" Nothing ever occurred afterward to dim his fame, and he is known in history as the Chevalier John Paul Jones."

Just here a passing vessel attracted the attention of the captain and the others, and it was not until some hours later that the conversation in regard to the doings of the navy was resumed.

CHAPTER XVII.

TOWARD evening the young people again gathered about the captain, asking that his story of naval exploits might be continued.

" I am not sure," he said pleasantly, " that to recount naval exploits is the wisest thing I can do ; it stirs my blood, and revives the old love for the service."

" Oh, Papa, please don't ever, ever go back to your ship and leave us ! " exclaimed Gracie, tears starting to her eyes at the very thought.

" I am not at all sure that I would be accepted should I offer my services again, my darling," he answered, drawing her into his arms and caressing her tenderly ; " but really I have no serious thought of so doing."

" Oh, I'm glad of that, you dear Papa ! " she said with a sigh of relief, putting her arm about his neck and kissing him with ardent affection.

" So am I," said Lulu. " I don't know what I would n't rather have happen than to be parted again for months and maybe years from my dear father."

A loving look was his reply as he drew her to his other side and caressed her with equal tenderness.

At that little Elsie came running toward them. "Me too, Papa," she said, "kiss me too, and let me sit on your knee while you tell 'bout things that happened a long while ago."

"Yes, the baby girl has the best right to sit on Papa's knee when she wants to," said Lulu, good-naturedly making way for the little one.

A loving look and smile from her father as he lifted the baby girl to the coveted seat and gave her the asked for caress, amply rewarded her little act of self-denial.

"I cannot begin to tell you to-day all the exploits of our navy even during the first war with England," the Captain said; "you will have to read the history for yourselves, and I trust will enjoy doing so, but I shall try to relate some of the more prominent incidents in a way to entertain you."

"What kind of flag did our naval vessels carry at the beginning of the Revolutionary War, Captain?" asked Evelyn. "It was not till 1777, if my memory serves me right, that our present flag was adopted by Congress."

"You are quite right," the Captain said, "and up to that time each vessel of the little Continental navy carried one of her own choosing; or rather each commander was allowed to choose a device to suit himself. It is claimed for John Paul Jones that he raised with his own hands the first flag of a regular American cruiser. The vessel was Hopkins's flag-ship the 'Alfred.' It was at Philadelphia, early in 1776 the banner was raised. It had a white field, with the words 'Liberty Tree' in the centre above a representation of a pine tree; beneath were the words, 'Appeal to God.'"

"Yes, sir; but did n't some one about that time raise a flag composed of thirteen stripes?" queried Eva.

"Quite true," replied the Captain, "and across it a rattlesnake; underneath that, the words, 'Don't Tread On Me.'

"Both Continental vessels and privateers were very successful, and by mid-summer of 1776 they had captured more than five hundred British soldiers. There was a Captain Conyngham, a brave and skilful seaman, who sailed from Dunkirk in May, 1777, in the brig 'Surprise,' under one of the commissions which Franklin carried with him to France for army and navy officers. (Those of you who have studied geography will, I suppose, remember that Dunkirk is in the north of France.) Conyngham was very successful; had in a few days captured the British packet ship 'Prince of Orange' and a brig, and returned with them to Dunkirk. The English ambassador at Paris complained very strongly, and to appease the wrath of the English, the French Government put the captain and his crew in prison."

" Oh, what a shame ! " cried Lulu.

Her father smiled slightly at that. " They were not kept there very long," he said, " but were soon released, and Conyngham allowed to fit out another cruiser, called the ' Revenge.' "

" A very suitable name," laughed Max.

" Yes," assented his father, and went on with his history. " The British Government had sent two vessels to arrest Conyngham and his men as pirates, but when they reached Dunkirk he had already sailed. Had the British succeeded in taking them, they would no doubt have been hanged as pirates ; for both Government and people of Great Britain were at that time much ex‑ asperated by the blows Americans were dealing their dearest interest, commerce. The Revenge ' was doing so much injury, — making prizes of merchantmen, and so putting money into the hands of the American commissioners for public use, — that the British were at their wit's end ; the people in the seaports were greatly alarmed, and insurance on cargoes went up to twenty-five per cent. Some of the British merchants sent out their goods in French vessels for greater se‑ curity, — so many of them, in fact, that at one time there were forty French vessels together in the Thames taking in cargoes.

" At that time British transports were engaged in carrying German troops across the Atlantic to fight the Americans. Conyngham was on the

look-out for these, but did not succeed in meet⸗
ing with any of them."

" Such a despicable business as it was for
George III. to hire those fellows to fight the
people here!" exclaimed Max. " I wish Conyngham had caught some of them. Papa, did n't
he at one time disguise his ship and take her into
an English port to refit?"

" So it is said," replied the Captain ; " it was
for repairs, after a storm. It is said also that
he obtained supplies at one time in an Irish
port."

" Did n't British ships take ours sometimes,
Papa?" asked Grace.

" Yes," he replied, " victory was not always
on the side of the Americans. The fast-sailing
British frigates captured many privateersmen and
merchantmen, and considering their great superiority of numbers it would have been strange
indeed had that not been the case. The war on
the ocean was very destructive to both parties ;
yet the Americans were, with reason, amazed and
delighted with their measure of success, astonish-
ing in proportion to the odds against them.

" During that year — 1776 — they had captured three hundred and forty British vessels ;
four had been burned, forty-five recaptured, and
eighteen released.

" It was in the fall of that year that Benedict
Arnold commanded some stirring naval operations

on Lake Champlain. In the previous spring the British had made preparations to invade the Champlain and Hudson valleys, hoping thus to effect a separation between New England and the other colonies which would naturally make it an easier task to conquer both sections.

" To ward off that threatened danger the Americans holding Ticonderoga and Crown Point — both on the lake as you will remember — constructed a small squadron, the command of which was given to Arnold, who knew more about naval affairs than any other available person. Three schooners, one sloop, and five gondolas were armed and manned, and with this little squadron Arnold sailed down to the foot of the lake and made observations.

" In the mean time the British had heard of what was going on, and they, too, had prepared a small squadron on the river Sorel, the outlet of the lake. Their navy consisted of twenty-four gun-boats, each armed with a field-piece or carriage-gun, and a large flat-bottomed boat called the ' Thunderer,' carrying heavy guns.

" It was not till the middle of October that the fight took place. Arnold, with his flotilla, was then lying between the western shore of the lake and Valcour Island. The ' Congress ' was his flagship. The British attacked him, and a very severe fight followed. It was brought to a conclusion only by the coming of a very dark night.

The Americans had lost the ' Royal Savage ' in the action ; the rest of the flotilla fled up the lake, eluding the British in the darkness.

" The next morning the British followed ; and all that day and the following night the chase continued. Early the next morning the British succeeded in coming up with the Americans, and another battle followed. Arnold, who was on the galley ' Congress,' fought hard until his vessel was nearly a wreck, then ran her and four others into a creek and set them on fire to prevent their falling into the hands of the foe.

" Those who were left of the crews escaped and made their way to Crown Point."

" Arnold did do good work for his country in the early part of the war," exclaimed Rosie. " If he had been killed in that fight he would always have been considered as great a patriot as any other man of the time."

" Yes," replied the Captain with an involuntary sigh, " if he had fallen then, or even some years later, his memory would have been as fondly cherished as that of almost any other soldier of the Revolution. He would have been considered one of the noblest champions of liberty. Ah, what a pity he should turn traitor and make himself the object of infamy, as lasting as the history of his native land, which he attempted to betray into the hands of her foes ! "

" Doubtless after years must have brought him

many an hour of bitter regret," said Mrs. Travilla, echoing the Captain's sigh. "Poor fellow! I hope he repented and was forgiven of God, though his countrymen could never forgive him. He had a pious mother who tried to train him up aright, and certainly must have often prayed earnestly for her son; so I hope he may have repented and found forgiveness and salvation through the atoning blood of Christ."

"I would be glad indeed to know that he had, Mamma," said Violet.

"I too," added the Captain. "I think he must have been a very wretched man in the latter years of his life."

"Was he treated well in England, Papa?" asked Lulu.

"Not by every one," replied her father; "some of the noble-minded there showed him very plainly that they despised him for his treason. George III. introduced him to Earl Balcarras, who had been with Burgoyne at the battle of Bemis's Heights; but the earl refused his hand, and turned on his heel saying, 'I know General Arnold, and abominate traitors.'"

"How Arnold must have felt that!" exclaimed Rosie. "I would not have liked to be in his shoes."

"Nor I," said her mother. "The British officers thoroughly despised him, and there is an anecdote of a meeting he once had with Talleyrand which must have been trying to his feelings, if he had any sense of honour left.

"It seems that Talleyrand, who was fleeing from France during the revolution there, inquired at the hotel where he was at the time, for some American who could give him letters of introduction to persons of influence here. He was told that an American gentleman was in an adjoining room. It seems it was Arnold, though no one, I suppose, knew who he was. Talleyrand sought an interview with him, and made his request for letters of introduction, when Arnold at once retreated from the room, as he did so saying with a look of pain on his face, ' I was born in America, lived there till the prime of my life, but, alas! I can call no man in America my friend.' "

" I should feel sorry for him in spite of that black act of treason," Violet said, "if he had not followed it up by such infamous deeds against his countrymen, even those of them who had been his neighbours and friends in his early years. I remember Lossing tells us that while New Haven — set on fire by Arnold's band of Tories and Hessians — was burning, he stood in the belfry of a church watching the conflagration with probably the same kind of satisfaction that Nero felt in the destruction of Rome. Think of such a murderous expedition against the home and friends of his childhood and youth! the wanton destruction of a thriving town ! It showed him to be a most malicious wretch, worthy of the scorn and contempt with which he was treated even by many of those who had profited by his treason."

" Yes ; ' the way of transgressors is hard,' " quoted her mother.

CHAPTER XVIII.

For some days the "Dolphin" rode at anchor in Bar Harbour, Mount Desert, while its passengers found great enjoyment in trips here and there about the island, visiting the Ovens, Otter Cliffs, Schooner Head, and other points of interest.

But the time was drawing near when Max must show himself to the examiners of applicants for cadetship in Annapolis, and early one bright morning, a favourable land breeze springing up, the yacht weighed anchor and started southward.

They were to touch at Newport on their way and take on board any of their party left there who might care to visit Annapolis with them.

As usual all gathered upon deck shortly after breakfast, and again the young people besieged the Captain with requests for something more about the doings of Revolutionary days.

"You know, Papa," said Lulu, "we've been so busy visiting all those lovely places on Mount Desert that we haven't had time for anything about the wars since you told us how Arnold fought the British on Lake Champlain."

"Yes, I remember," he said. "How would you like now to hear of some of the doings and happenings of those times in and about Newport?"

"Oh, please do tell of them! We'd like it ever so much," answered several young voices, and the Captain good-naturedly complied.

"I will begin," he said, "with a bold and brave exploit of Major Silas Talbot, in the fall of 1778. The British had converted a strong vessel into a galley, named it the 'Pigot,' in honour of their general of that name, and anchored it in the channel between the eastern side of the island bearing the same name as the State, and the main land. It was armed with twelve eight-pounders and ten swivels, making a formidable floating battery, the object of which was to close up the channel against the French fleet which lay off Newport.

"It also effectually broke up the local trade of that section; therefore its destruction was very desirable, and Major Talbot proposed to head an expedition to accomplish that, or its capture. General Sullivan thought the thing could not be done, but finally gave consent that the effort should be made.

"Sixty resolute patriots were drafted for the purpose and on the 10th of October they set sail in a coasting-sloop called the 'Hawk,' armed with only three three-pounders, beside the small arms carried by the men.

" They passed the British forts at Bristol Ferry and anchored within a few miles of the ' Pigot.' Major Talbot then procured a horse, rode down the east bank and reconnoitred. He saw that the ' Pigot ' presented a formidable appearance, but he was not too much alarmed thereby to make the proposed attempt to capture her.

" At nine o'clock that same evening he hoisted his anchor, and favoured by a fair wind, started on his perilous errand. He had with him Lieutenant Helm, of Rhode Island, with a small reinforcement. He had also a kedge-anchor, lashed to his jib-boom, with which to tear the nettings of the ' Pigot.' The darkness of the night enabled him to drift past Fogland Ferry Fort under bare poles, without being discovered; he then hoisted sail and ran partly under the stern of the ' Pigot.'

" The sentinels hailed him, but no answer was returned; and they fired a volley of musketry at the ' Hawk,' which fortunately hit no one, while her kedge-anchor tore the ' Pigot's ' nettings and grappled her, and so gave the Americans a free passage to her deck. They poured on it from the ' Hawk,' with loud shouts, and drove every man from the deck except the captain. He, in shirt and drawers, fought desperately till he found that resistance was useless, when he surrendered his vessel with the officers and crew.

"The Americans secured the prisoners below by coiling the cables over the hatchways, weighed anchor, and started for the harbour of Stonington, which they entered the next day with their prize."

"Good!" cried Max. "I'd have liked to be one of those brave fellows, and I hope Congress rewarded them for their gallant deed."

"It did," said the Captain; "presented Talbot with a commission of lieutenant-colonel in the army of the United States, and complimented both him and his men."

"I suppose they'd have given them some money if they'd had it to spare," remarked Lulu; "but of course they hadn't, because the country was so dreadfully poor then."

"Yes," said her father, "it was poor, and Newport, Rhode Island, was suffering greatly from the long-continued occupation of the British. The people of that colony had from the first taken a bold and determined stand in opposition to the usurpations of King George and his ministers, and the oppressions of their tools in this country.

"In the summer of 1769 a British armed sloop, sent there by the commissioners of customs, lay in Narragansett Bay, she was called 'Liberty,' certainly a most inappropriate name. Her errand was similar to that of the 'Gaspee' about the destruction of which I have already told you, — though that occurred some three years later. The commander of the ' Liberty,' was a Captain Reid. A schooner and brig belonging to Connecticut had been seized and brought into Newport ; also the clothing and the sword of the captain, Packwood, commander of the brig, had been taken, and carried aboard the ' Liberty.' He went there to recover them, was badly maltreated, and as he left the sloop in his boat, was fired upon with a musket and a brace of pistols.

" This occurrence greatly exasperated the people of Newport, who demanded of Reid that the man who had fired upon Captain Packwood should be sent ashore.

" Reid again and again sent the wrong man, which of course exasperated the people, and they determined to show him that they were not to be trifled with. Accordingly, a number of them boarded the ' Liberty,' cut her cables, and set her adrift. The tide carried her down the bay and drifted her to Goat Island, where the people, after throwing her stores and ammunition into the water, scuttled her, and set her on fire. Her boats were dragged to the common, and burned there."

" Was she entirely burned, Papa?" asked Gracie.

" Almost, after burning for several days."

"And that was nearly six years before the battle of Lexington," Evelyn remarked in a half musing tone. "How wonderfully patient and forbearing the Americans were, putting up for years with so much of British insolence and oppression!"

"I think they were," responded the Captain. "Nor was it from cowardice, as they plainly showed when once war with Great Britain was fairly inaugurated.

"And the little State of Rhode Island had her full share in the struggle and the suffering it brought. Let us see what Bancroft says in regard to the action of her citizens at the beginning of the conflict, immediately after the battles of Lexington and Concord," he added, taking up and opening a book lying near at hand. All waited in silence as he turned over the leaves and began to read, —

"The nearest towns of Rhode Island were in motion before the British had finished their retreat. At the instance of Hopkins and others, Wanton, the governor, though himself inclined to the royal side, called an assembly. Its members were all of one mind; and when Wanton, with several of the council, showed hesitation, they resolved, if necessary, to proceed alone. The council yielded and confirmed the unanimous vote of the assembly for raising an army of fifteen hundred men. 'The colony of Rhode Island,' wrote Bowler, the speaker, to the Massachusetts congress, 'is firm and determined; and a greater unanimity in the lower house scarce ever prevailed.' Companies of the men of Rhode Island preceded this early message."

"The little State took a noble stand," remarked Violet, as her husband finished reading and closed the book.

"Yes," he said, "and their consequent sufferings from British aggressions promptly began. Admiral Wallace, an inhuman wretch, that summer commanded a small British fleet lying in Newport harbour. It was he who promised to hang Abraham Whipple, but never caught him. It was discovered by the Americans that he (Wallace) was planning to carry off the live-stock from the lower end of the island to supply the British army at Boston."

"Going to steal them, Papa?" asked Gracie.

"Yes; but the people were too quick for him. Some of them went down one dark night in September and brought off a thousand sheep and fifty head of cattle; and three hundred minute-men drove a good many more to Newport, so saving them from being taken by Wallace and his men.

"Wallace was very angry, ordered the people to make contributions to supply his fleet with provisions, and to force them to do so took care to prevent them from getting their usual supplies of fuel and provisions from the mainland.

"The people were much alarmed, and about half of them left the town. Shortly afterward a treaty was made by which they engaged to supply the fleet with provisions and beer, and Wallace allowed them to move about as they pleased. But soon, however, he demanded three hundred sheep of the people of Bristol, and upon their refusal to comply, bombarded their town.

"He began the bombardment about eight o'clock in the evening. The rain was pouring in torrents; and the poor women and children fled through the darkness and storm, out to the open fields to escape from the flying shot and shell of the invaders."

" Oh, how dreadful for the poor things ! " exclaimed Gracie.

"Yes, there was great suffering among them," replied her father. "The house of Governor Bradford was burned, as also were many others. Wallace played the pirate in Narragansett Bay for a month, wantonly destroying the people's property, seizing every American vessel that entered Newport harbour and sending it to Boston, — which, as you will remember, was then occupied by the British general, Gage, and his troops, — plundering and burning all the dwellings on the beautiful island of Providence, and all the buildings near the ferry at Canonicut.

"He kept possession of the harbour till the

spring of 1776 ; but in April of that year some American troops came to try to drive him away. Captain Grimes brought two row-galleys, each carrying two eighteen-pounders, from Providence. Provincial troops brought two more eighteen-pounders and planted them on shore where the British, who were anchored about a mile above Newport, could see them.

" Wallace evidently thought the danger too great and immediate, for he weighed anchor, and with his whole squadron sailed out of the harbour without firing a shot."

" He must have been a coward like most men who revel in such cruelty," remarked Max sagely. " Not much like the Wallace of Scotland who fought the English so bravely in early times."

" I quite agree with you in that thought, Max," his father said with a slight smile. " This Wallace was the same who, later in the war, plundered and destroyed the property of the Americans on the Hudson, desolating the farms of innocent men because they preferred freedom to the tyrannical rule of the English government, and laying the town of Kingston in ashes.

" Soon after he sailed out of Narragansett Bay another British vessel called the ' Glasgow,' carrying twenty-nine guns, came into the harbour and anchored near Fort Island. She had just come out of a severe fight with some American vessels, held the same day that Wallace left

Newport. Probably her officers thought he was still there so that their vessel would be safe in that harbour, but they soon discovered their mistake. The Americans threw up a breast-work on Brenton's Point, placed some pieces of heavy artillery there, and the next morning opened upon her and another vessel so vigorous a fire from their battery that they soon cut their cables and went out to sea again."

CHAPTER XIX.

"Had the land troops of the British gone away also, Captain?" asked Evelyn.

"No," he replied. "Early in May the British troops left the houses of the town and returned to their camp. It was some relief to the poor, outraged people whose dwellings had been turned into noisy barracks, their pleasant groves, beautiful shade-trees and broad forests destroyed, their property taken from them, their wives and children exposed to the profanity, low ribaldry, and insults of the ignorant and brutal soldiery; but there was by no means entire relief; they were still plundered and insulted.

"Clinton had gone to New York with about one half the troops, but a far worse tyrant held command in his place, Major-General Prescott by name; he was a dastardly coward when in danger, the meanest of petty tyrants when he felt it safe to be such, narrow minded, hard hearted and covetous, — anything but a gentleman. A more unfit man for the place could hardly have been found.

"When he saw persons conversing together as he walked the streets, he would shake his cane

at them and call out, ' Disperse, ye rebels! '
Also, he would command them to take off their
hats to him, and unless his order was instantly
obeyed, enforce it by a rap with his cane."

" That must have been hard indeed to bear,"
remarked Violet.

" Yes," cried Max hotly. " I 'd have enjoyed
knocking him down."

" Probably better than the consequences of
your act," laughed his father; then went on :
" Prescott was passing out of town one evening,
going to his country quarters, when he overtook
a Quaker, who of course did not doff his hat.
Prescott was on horseback ; he dashed up to the
Quaker, pressed him up against a stone wall,
knocked off his hat, and then put him under
guard.

"He imprisoned many citizens of Newport without giving any reason. One was a man named
William Tripp, a very respectable citizen, who
had a wife and a large and interesting family,
with none of whom was he allowed to hold any
communication.

" But Tripp's wife had contrivance enough
to open a correspondence with her husband by
sending him a loaf of bread with a letter baked
in the inside. Whether he could find means to
send a reply I do not know, but it must have
been some consolation to hear from her and his
children.

"While Tripp was still in prison she tried to see Prescott, to beg that her husband might be set free, or she allowed a personal interview with him. She was told to come again the next day. Her application had been made to a Captain Savage, the only person through whom she might hope to gain the coveted interview with Prescott ; but when she again went to him, at the appointed time, he treated her very roughly, refusing her request to see the general, and as he shut the door violently in her face, telling her with fiendish exultation that he expected her husband would be hung as a rebel in less than a week."

"Truly, his was a most appropriate name," remarked Grandma Elsie.

"And did they hang the poor man, Papa?" asked Gracie.

"I do not know, my darling," he answered, "but I hope not. Would you all like to hear something more about his persecutor, Prescott?"

"Yes, sir, yes," came promptly from several young voices.

"You may be sure," the Captain went on, "that the people of Newport grew very tired of their oppressor, and devised various plans for ridding themselves of him. None of these proved successful, but at length a better one was contrived and finally carried out by Lieutenant-Colonel Barton, of Providence. Lossing speaks of it as one of the boldest and most hazardous enterprizes undertaken during the war. It was accomplished on the night of the 10th of July, 1777.

"At that time Prescott was quartered at the house of a Quaker named Overing, about five miles above Newport, on the west road leading to the ferry, at the north part of the island.

"Barton's plan was to cross the bay under cover of the darkness, seize Prescott, and carry him off to the American camp. But it was a very dangerous thing to attempt, because three British frigates, with their guard-boats, were lying in the bay almost in front of Overing's house. But taking with him a few chosen men, in four whale-boats, with muffled oars, Barton embarked from Warwick Point at nine o'clock, passed silently between the islands of Prudence and Patience over to Rhode Island, hearing on the way the cry of the British sentries from their guard-boats, 'All's well.'

"They — the Americans — landed in Codding-ton's Cove, at the mouth of a small stream which passed by Overing's. Barton divided his men into several squads, and assigned to each its station and duty. Then in the strictest order and profound silence they made their way to the house, the larger portion of them passing be-tween a British guard-house and the encampment of a company of light-horse, while the rest of the party were to reach the same point by a circuitous route, approaching it from the rear, then to secure the doors.

"As Barton and his men drew near the gate they were hailed by a sentinel stationed there. He hailed them twice, and then demanded the countersign. Barton answered, 'We have no countersign to give,' then quickly asked, 'Have you seen any deserters here to-night?'

"That query allayed the sentinel's suspicions, so putting him off his guard, and the next moment he found himself seized, bound, and threatened with instant death if he attempted to give the alarm.

"While Barton and his party had been thus engaged the division from the rear had secured the doors, and Barton now walked boldly into the front passage and on into a room where he found Mr. Overing, seated alone, reading, the rest of the family having already retired to their beds.

"Barton asked for General Prescott's room, and Overing silently pointed to the ceiling, intimating that it was directly overhead. Barton then walked quietly up the stairs, four strong white men and a powerful negro named Sisson, accompanying him. He gently tried Prescott's door, but found it locked. There was no time to be lost; the negro drew back a couple of paces, and using his head for a battering-ram, burst open the door at the first effort.

"Prescott, who was in bed, thought the intruders were robbers, and springing out, seized his gold watch which hung upon the wall. But Barton, gently laying a hand on his shoulder, said, 'You are my prisoner, sir, and perfect silence is your only safety.'

"Prescott asked to be allowed to dress, but Barton refused, saying there was not time; for he doubtless felt that every moment of delay was dangerous to himself and his companions, and as it was a hot July night there was no need for his prisoner to fear taking cold. He therefore threw a cloak about him, placed him and his *aide*, Major Barrington (who, hearing a noise in the general's room, had taken the alarm and leaped from a window to make his escape, but only to be captured by the Americans) between two armed men, hurried them to the shore where the boats were in waiting, and quickly carried them over the water to Warwick Point. When they reached there Prescott ventured to break the silence that had been imposed upon him by saying to Colonel Barton, 'Sir, you have made a bold push to-night.'

"'We have been fortunate,' replied Barton coolly.

"Prescott and Barrington were then placed in a coach which Captain Elliott had waiting there for them, and taken to Providence, arriving there about sunrise."

" I wonder," remarked Lulu, " if Prescott received the harsh treatment from our men that he deserved."

" No," replied her father, " I am proud to be able to say that American officers rarely, if ever, treated their prisoners with anything like the harshness and cruelty usually dealt out by the British to theirs. Prescott was kindly treated by General Spencer and his officers, and shortly after his capture was sent to Washington's headquarters at Middlebrook, on the Raritan.

" But it seems that at a tavern on the way he received something better suited to his deserts. At Lebanon a Captain Alden kept a tavern, and there Prescott and his escort stopped to dine. While they were at the table Mrs. Alden brought on a dish of succotash."

" What's that, Papa ? " queried little Elsie, who had climbed to her favourite seat upon her father's knee.

" Corn and beans boiled together," he replied ; " a dish that is quite a favourite with most people in that part of the country ; but was, I presume, quite new to Prescott, and he exclaimed indignantly, ' What ! do you treat me with the food of hogs ? ' Then taking the dish from the table he strewed its contents over the floor.

" Some one presently carried the news of his doings to Captain Alden, and he walked into the dining-room armed with a horse-whip and gave Prescott a severe flogging."

" I think it served him right," remarked Lulu, " for his insolence, and for wasting good food that somebody else would have been glad to eat."

" Prescott must surely have been very badly brought up," said Rosie, " and was anything but a gentleman. I pity the poor Newport people if he was ever restored to his command there. Was he, brother Levis? I really have quite forgotten."

" Unfortunately for them, he was," replied the Captain. " He was exchanged for General Charles Lee the next April, and returned to his former command.

" While he was still there the Newport people sent a committee — Timothy Folger, William Rotch and Dr. Tupper — to him to arrange some matters concerning the town. They found some difficulty in gaining an interview; and when at length Folger and the doctor succeeded in so doing, Prescott stormed so violently at the former that he was compelled to withdraw.

" After the doctor had told his errand and Prescott had calmed down, he asked, ' Was n't my treatment of Folger very uncivil?'

" The doctor answered in the affirmative, and Prescott went on to say, ' I will tell you the reason; he looked so much like a Connecticut man that horse-whipped me that I could not endure his presence.' "

CHAPTER XX.

THERE was time for only a brief stay in the cottages near Newport before the "Dolphin" must sail for Annapolis, in order that Max might be there in season for the examination of applicants for cadetship in the United States Navy. He had not changed his mind, but was looking forward with delight to the life that seemed to be opening before him; for he loved the sea, and thought no profession could be more honourable than that chosen by his father, who was in his eyes the impersonation of all that was noble, good, and wise.

He was not sorry that his suspense in regard to acceptance would soon be ended, though both he and the other young people of the party would have liked to visit places in the neighbourhood of Newport made memorable by the occurrence of events in the Revolutionary War; but the Captain encouraged the hope that they would all be able to do so at some future time; also said they would find at Annapolis some souvenirs of the struggle for independence quite as well worth attention as those they were for the present leaving behind.

So they started upon their southward way in excellent spirits, Mr. and Mrs. Dinsmore accompanying them.

On the first evening of their renewed voyage the young people gathered around the Captain and begged for some account of Revolutionary occurrences in the State they were now about to visit.

"I will go back a little further than that," he said pleasantly, drawing Gracie to a seat upon his knee, — "to the action of the people of Maryland upon hearing of the passage of the Stamp Act. In August, 1765, there was a meeting at Annapolis of the 'Assertors of British American privileges' held 'to show their detestation of and abhorrence to some late tremendous attacks on liberty, and their dislike to a certain late arrived officer, a *native of this province.*'

"The person to whom they referred was a Mr. Hood, who had been appointed stamp-master while in England shortly before. Dr. Franklin had recommended him for the place; but the people were so angry that no one would buy goods of him, though offered at a very low price. He learned that they intended to give him a coat of tar and feathers, but escaped to New York in time to save himself from that.

"As they could n't catch him they made an effigy of him, dressed it oddly, put it in a cart, like a malefactor, with some sheets of paper before it, and paraded it through the town, the bell tolling all the while. They then took it to a hill, punished it at the whipping-post and pillory, hung it on the gibbet, then set fire to a tar-barrel underneath and burned it."

" Oh," gasped Gracie, " how dreadful if it had been the man himself ! "

" But it was n't, Gracie dear," laughed Lulu; " and if it had been, I 'm not sure it was worse than he deserved."

" But I suppose they had to use the stamps for all that, — had n't they?" asked Rosie.

" The people refused to use them, and for a time all business was at an end," said the Captain, going on with his narrative. " Governor Sharpe sent back some of the stamped paper which arrived in December, informing the colonial secretary of the proceedings of the people, and said that if they got hold of any stamped paper they would be pretty sure to burn it.

" On the 31st of October the ' Maryland Gazette ' appeared in mourning, and said, ' The times are Dreadful, Dismal, Doleful, Dolorous and Dollarless.' On the 10th of December the editor issued ' an apparition of the late " Maryland Gazette," ' and expressed his opinion that the odious Stamp Act would never be carried into effect.

" There was great rejoicing when the intelligence reached Annapolis that the Act had been repealed. There were many manifestations of mirth and festivity; but, as you all know, that rejoicing was short-lived, for the king and his ministers continued their aggressions upon the liberties of the American people.

" In the autumn of 1774 the people of Annapolis were greatly excited over the Boston Port Bill, and ripe for rebellion. They also resolved that no tea should be landed on their shores; and when on Saturday, October 15, the ship 'Peggy,' Captain Stewart, arrived from London, bringing among other things, seventeen packages of tea, the citizens were summoned to a general meeting.

" It was the first arrival of tea since it had become a proscribed article. It was ascertained that it was consigned to T. C. Williams & Co., of Annapolis, that they had imported it, and that Antony Stewart, proprietor of the vessel, had paid the duty on it. This the meeting looked upon as an acknowledgement of the right claimed by King and Parliament to tax the tea brought to the colonies, and it was resolved not to permit the tea to be landed.

" The people of the surrounding country were summoned to a meeting in the city, to be held on the following Wednesday. Mr. Stewart published a handbill of explanation of his connection with the affair, saying that he had no intention of violating the non-importation pledges, and regretted that the article had been placed on board his ship.

"But the people had been deceived on former occasions, and knew that when men got into trouble they were apt to whine and pretend innocence; therefore they were more disposed to punish than forgive Mr. Stewart, and at their Wednesday meeting resolved to destroy the vessel with its packages of tea.

"But Mr. Stewart, by the advice of some of his friends, decided to destroy the vessel and the tea himself, and did so. He ran the ship aground near Windmill Point and set her on fire. That satisfied the people and the crowd dispersed.

"A historian of the time says, 'the destruction of tea at Boston has acquired renown as an act of unexampled daring, but the tea burning of Annapolis, which occurred the ensuing fall, far surpassed it in the apparent deliberation, and utter carelessness of concealment, attending the bold measures which led to its accomplishment.'"

"Did the Americans hold any other such 'tea parties,' Papa?" asked Lulu with a humorous look.

"Yes," he said; "in New York and New Jersey; but I will reserve the stories of those doings for another time, and go on now with what occurred in Maryland, — principally at Annapolis, — in the times now under consideration.

" There was a small tea-burning at Elizabeth-town — now called Hagerstown, — the Committee of Vigilance obliging a man named John Parks to go with his hat off and a lighted torch in his hand and set fire to a chest of tea in his possession. The committee also recommended entire non-intercourse with Parks; but that did not seem sufficient to the people, and they added to it the breaking of his doors and windows. It is said too, that tar and feathers were freely used in various places.

" Maryland was not ready quite so soon as some of the other colonies to declare herself free and independent; but Charles Carroll, William Paca, Samuel Chase, and others, called county conventions, and used their influence to persuade their fellow-citizens of the wisdom and necessity of such a course, and on the 28th of June, the Maryland Convention empowered their delegates to concur with the other colonies in a declaration of independence.

" As you all know, that declaration was drawn up and signed by Congress shortly afterward, and the men whose names I have mentioned were all among the signers."

" Was there any fighting in or about Annapolis, Papa?" asked Lulu.

" No," he said, " but it was frequently the scene of military displays."

" I 'd have liked that a great deal better if I

had been there," remarked Gracie. " But won't you please tell us about them, Papa? "

" I will," he answered, smiling upon her and softly smoothing her hair. " Washington passed through Annapolis on his way northward after the battle of Yorktown, which, as you will all remember, virtually ended our struggle for independence, though there was still fighting going on in different parts of the country. Business was suspended in Annapolis when Washington was known to be coming, and the people crowded streets and windows to gain a sight of the chief as he passed. A public address was made him, and everything done to show their appreciation, respect, and esteem.

" Again he was there when, the war at an end, he resigned his commission as commander-in-chief of the American forces.

" ' The State House at Annapolis, now venerated because of the associations which cluster around it, was filled with the brave, the fair, and the patriotic of Maryland, to witness the sublime spectacle of that beloved chief resigning his military power wielded with such mighty energy and glorious results for eight long years into the hands of the civil authority which gave it,' says Lossing."

" But why did Washington go to Maryland to do that, Papa? " asked Gracie.

" Because the Continental Congress was then

in session there," replied her father. " It was a most interesting scene which then took place in the Senate Chamber of the Capitol. The time was noon of the 23d of December, 1783. Beside the congressmen there were present the governor, council and legislature of Maryland, general officers, and the representative of France. Places were assigned to all these, while spectators filled the galleries and crowded the floor.

" Bancroft tells us that ' rising with dignity, Washington spoke of the rectitude of the common cause ; the support of Congress ; of his countrymen ; of Providence ; and he commended the interests of our dearest country to the care of Almighty God. Then saying that he had finished the work assigned him to do, he bade an affectionate farewell to the august body under whose orders he had so long acted, resigned with satisfaction the commission which he had accepted with diffidence, and took leave of public life. His emotion was so great that, as he advanced and delivered up his commission, he seemed unable to have uttered more.'

" Washington still stood while the president of Congress, turning pale from emotion, made a short address in reply, only a sentence or two of which I will quote : " —

" Having taught a lesson useful to those who inflict and those who feel oppression, with the blessings of your fellow-citizens you retire from the great field of action; but the glory of your virtues will continue to animate remotest ages. We join you in commending the interests of our dearest country to the protection of Almighty God, beseeching him to dispose the hearts and minds of its citizens to improve the opportunity afforded them of becoming a happy and respectable nation."

" Which I think we have become," added Max, with satisfaction, as his father paused in his narrative.

" By God's blessing upon the work of our pious forefathers," added the Captain, with a look of mingled gratitude and pride in the land of his birth.

" I think we must all visit the State House when in Annapolis," remarked Grandma Elsie, who sat near and had been listening with almost as keen interest as that shown by the younger ones.

" Certainly we must," said Mr. Dinsmore. " Some of us have been there before, but a second visit will not prove uninteresting, especially along with the young folks, to whom it will be quite new," and he glanced smilingly around upon the bright, eager faces.

His suggestion was followed by expressions of pleasure in the prospect. Then the Captain was besieged with entreaties that he would go on with his account of things of historical interest to be found in Annapolis.

" There is the little gallery in which Mrs.
Washington and other ladies stood to witness the
scene I have tried to describe," he continued. " It
is said to be unchanged, as are also the doors, windows, cornices, and other architectural belongings.
I confess it sent a thrill through me when I first
saw them all, to think they were the very same
which echoed the voice of the Father of his Country on that memorable occasion.

" Also the very spot where Mifflin, the president, and Thomson, the secretary, of Congress
sat when the treaty of peace with Great Britain
was ratified, can be pointed out to the interested
observer, which I certainly was."

" It is a fine building," remarked Mr. Dinsmore, " much admired for its style of architecture
and the beauty of its situation."

" It is indeed," assented the Captain. " It is
built of brick, has a fine dome, surmounted by
two smaller ones, with a cupola of wood. As
it stands upon an elevation in the centre of the
city, there is a magnificent prospect from its
dome. One sees the city and harbour, while far
away to the southeast stretches Chesapeake Bay,
with Kent Island and the eastern shore looming
up in the distance."

" I remember two incidents which I have
heard were connected with the building of that
State House," remarked Mrs. Dinsmore. " One
is, that when the corner-stone was laid by

Governor Eden, just as he struck it with a mallet a severe clap of thunder burst over the city out of a clear sky ; the other, that the man who executed the stucco-work of the dome, fell from the scaffold and was killed just as he had completed his centre-piece."

" Yes," the Captain said, " I have heard those incidents were traditional, but am not able to vouch for their truth."

"Is there not a portrait of Washington there?" asked Violet.

" Yes," replied her husband, " in the House of Delegates ; it is a full-length likeness, and he is attended by La Fayette and Colonel Tilghman, the Continental army passing in review. It was painted by Peale as commemorative of the surrender at Yorktown, having been ordered by the Assembly of Maryland.

" There are also full-length portraits of Carroll, Stone, Paca, and Chase on the walls of the Senate Chamber. The first two were painted by Sully, the other two by Bordley, — both native artists. There is also a full-length portrait of William Pitt, Earl of Chatham, in Roman costume. Peale painted that also, and presented it to Maryland, his native State, in 1794. The work was done in England, and is of a high order.

" The only other portrait I recollect as being there is one of John Eager Howard, who, you doubtless remember, was one of the heroes of the Revolution."

Favourable winds and weather enabled the "Dolphin" to reach her destination a day or two earlier than the Captain had expected, so giving our party a little more time for sight-seeing than they had hoped for. They made good use of it, going about and visiting all the places of interest. Almost the first that received their attention was the State House, with its mementos of the Revolutionary days, of which the Captain had been telling them.

They lingered long over the portraits and in the Senate Chamber, where the Father of his Country had resigned his commission as commander-in-chief of the Continental armies.

They ascended to the cupola also, and gazed with delight upon the beautiful landscape spread out at their feet, — Max manifesting great interest in the vessels lying in the harbour, particularly the practice-ship "Constellation" and the school-ship "Santee," and scarcely less in the monitor "Passaic" and the steam-sloop "Wyoming," swinging at their anchorage in the river.

"Papa, can I visit them?" he asked.

"Yes, my boy, I hope to take you to see them all," was the pleasant-toned reply. "I intend that you and all the party shall see everything that is worth their attention."

"That's very kind of you, Captain," remarked

Evelyn in a lively tone. "I for one am very desirous to see the Naval Academy, its grounds and the drills, — one at least. I so enjoyed seeing those on Gardiner's Island."

"You shall," replied the Captain, with his pleasant smile. "It will give me pleasure to take any of you who wish to go."

"I think that will be all of us," remarked Violet, with a bright and happy glance up into her husband's face.

They were descending the stairs as they talked, and presently had all passed out into the State House grounds. There they met a gentleman in undress naval uniform who, coming forward with a look of extreme pleasure, warmly grasped the hand of Captain Raymond, calling him by name, and saying, "I do not know when I have had so agreeable a surprise."

The Captain returned the salutation as warmly as it was given, then introduced the rest of his party, telling them that this friend of his was commander-commandant of cadets.

At that Max's eyes opened very wide and fixed themselves upon the gentleman with as eager interest as if he had been a king.

Captain Raymond noted it with a look of mingled amusement and pride in the lad.

"This is my son Max, sir, a candidate for cadetship," he said, laying a hand affectionately upon Max's shoulder, "and I see he is much interested in this his first sight of one who will, he hopes, soon be his commander."

" Ah! a son of yours, Raymond? But I might have guessed it from his striking likeness to his father," the commandant said in a pleased and interested tone, grasping the boy's hand warmly as he spoke. " I have little doubt that he will pass," he added with a smile, " for he should inherit a good mind, and he looks bright and intelligent, — his father's son mentally as well as physically."

Max coloured with pleasure. " It is exactly what I want to be, sir," he said, — " as like my father as possible." And his eyes sought that father's face with a look of love and reverence that was pleasant to see.

The Captain met it with a smile of fatherly affection. " One's children are apt to be partial judges," he said ; then changing the subject of conversation, he stated the desire of those under his escort to see the Naval Academy and the Naval vessels lying at anchor in the harbour.

The commandant, saying he had some hours at his disposal, undertook to be their escort ; and thus they saw everything under the most favourable auspices.

The drill of the artillery battalion seemed to Max and Lulu very similar to that they had witnessed at West Point, but was scarcely the less exciting and interesting. They watched it all with sparkling eyes and eager, animated looks, Max hoping soon to take part in it, and not at all regretting his choice of a profession. He was not a bashful lad, though by no means conceited or forward, and his father had assured him that if he retained his self-possession, not giving way to nervousness or fright, he was fully competent to pass.

The boy had unbounded confidence in his father's word, which helped him to so fully retain his self-possession that he found little or no difficulty in answering every question put to him, — for the Captain had been very careful to drill him perfectly, making him thorough in all the branches required, — and passed most successfully.

He was also pronounced by the examining physician physically sound and of robust constitution. He was accepted, took the oath of allegiance, and felt himself several inches taller than before.

Captain Raymond attended to all the business matters, saw the room and room-mate selected for his son, and did all that could be done to secure the boy's comfort and welfare. The parting from Mamma Vi, his sisters, and baby brother was quite hard for the lad's affectionate heart, but he managed to go through it almost without shedding tears, though one or two would come when Gracie clung weeping about his neck; but the last, the final farewell to his father, was hardest of all. In vain he reminded himself that it was not a final separation, that he might hope for long visits at home at some future time, that letters would pass frequently between them, and a visit be paid him now and then by that dearly loved, honoured, and revered parent ; just now he could only remember that the daily, hourly intercourse he had found so delightful was over, probably forever in this world.

The Captain read it all in his boy's speaking countenance, and deeply sympathized with his son ; indeed his own heart was heavy over the thought that this, his first-born and well-beloved child was now to pass from under his protecting care and try the world for himself. He felt that he must bestow upon him a few more words of loving, fatherly counsel.

They were leaving together the hotel where the remainder of their party were domiciled for the present. " Max, my son," he said kindly, looking at his watch as he spoke, " we have still more than an hour to spend as we like before you must be at the Academy. Shall we spend it on board the yacht?"

" Yes, sir, if you can spare the time to me," answered the lad, making a great effort to speak brightly and cheerfully.

" Then we will go there," the Captain said, giving his son an affectionate look and smile. " I

can find no better use for the next hour than de-
voting it to a little talk with my first-born, on
whom I have built so many hopes."

A few minutes later they were sitting side by
side in the "Dolphin's" cabin, no human creature near to see or overhear what might pass between them.

For a little while there was silence, each busy
with his own thoughts. It was Max who ended
it at last.

"Papa," he said brokenly, his hand creeping
into his father's, "you — you have been such a
good, *good* father to me; and — and I want to
be a credit and comfort to you. I" —

But there he broke down completely, and the
next moment — neither ever knew exactly how it
came about — he was sobbing in his father's arms.

"I — I wish I'd been a better boy, Papa," he
went on, "it 'most breaks my heart to think
now of the pain and trouble I've given you at
times."

"My boy, my dear, dear boy," the Captain
said in moved tones, pressing the lad to his
heart, "you have been a great joy and comfort
to me for years past, and words would fail me to
tell how dear you are to your father's heart. It
seems scarely longer ago than yesterday that I
first held my dear boy in my arms, and prayed
God that if his life was spared he might grow up
into a good, useful, Christian man, a blessing

to his parents, to the church, and to the world. Oh, my boy, never be afraid or ashamed to own yourself one who fears God and tries to keep his commandments, who loves Jesus, trusts in Him for salvation from sin and death, and tries to honour Him in all his words and ways. Strive to keep very near to the Master, Max, and to honour Him in all things. Never be ashamed to own yourself His disciple, His servant, and Him as your Lord and King. Remember His words, ' Whosoever therefore shall be ashamed of me and of my words, in this adulterous and sinful generation, of him shall also the Son of man be ashamed when He cometh in the glory of His Father with the holy angels.' Doubtless it will at times bring the ridicule of your companions upon you, but he is only a coward who can not bear that when undeserved ; and what is it compared to Christ's sufferings on the cross for you?"

" Oh, Papa, nothing, nothing at all compared to what Jesus bore for me! He will give me strength to be faithful in confessing Him before men, and your prayers will help me, too."

" Yes, my boy, and you may be sure that you will be ever on your father's heart, which will be often going up in prayer to God for a blessing on his absent son. It is to me a joyful thought that He is the hearer and answerer of prayer, and will be ever near my son, to keep him in the hour of trial and temptation, though I may know nothing of his danger or distress.

" Let us kneel down now and ask Him to be your guard and guide through all life's journey, to help you to be His faithful servant in all things, and to bring you safe to heaven at last."

They knelt side by side, and in a few well chosen words the Captain commended his beloved son to the care, the guardianship, and the guidance of the God of his fathers, asking that he might be a faithful follower of Jesus through all life's journey, and afterward spend an eternity of bliss in that happy land where sin and sorrow and partings are never known.

A hearty embrace followed, some few more words of fatherly counsel and advice, then they left the vessel, wended their way to the Naval Academy and parted for the time, the Captain comforting the heart of the more than half homesick lad with the promise of a visit from him at no very distant day and frequent letters in the mean time.

The " Dolphin " was to sail northward again that evening ; and as Max watched his father out of sight it required a mighty effort to keep back the tears from his eyes at the thought that he should behold that noble form and dearly loved face no more for months or — " Oh, who could say that some accident might not rob him forever of his best and dearest earthly friend? "

But he struggled with himself, turned reso-
lutely about, and entered into lively chat with
some of his new comrades, all the while the
cheering thought in his heart that nothing could
separate him from the presence and loving care of
his heavenly Father ; also that he surely would
be permitted, before many months had passed,
to see again the dear earthly one he so loved
and honoured. And in the meanwhile he was
resolved to do everything in his power to win
that father's approbation, and make him proud
and happy in his first-born son.

THE END.

If you are interested in continuing in the
Elsie Dinsmore Collection,
Book 17
or desire a catalog

send a self-stamped addressed envelope to:

Sovereign Grace Publishers, Inc.
P.O. Box 4998
Lafayette, IN 47903
Phone: (765) 429-4122
Fax: (765) 429-4142

FAMILY LINEAGE

HORACE
HORACE DINSMORE SR.
HORACE DINSMORE JR. (ELSIE'S FATHER)
HORACE HOWARD (NEPHEW)

ELSIE
ELSIE GRAYSON DINSMORE
ELSIE DINSMORE TRAVILLA (ELSIE'S DAUGHTER)
ELSIE TRAVILLA (DAUGHTER OF E.D.T.)

ROSE
ROSE ALLISON DINSMORE
ROSE DINSMORE (DAUGHTER)
ROSE TRAVILLA (GRANDDAUGHTER TO R.A.D.)
ROSE HOWARD (NIECE TO R.A.D.)

EDWARD
EDWARN TRAVILLA SR.
EDWARD TRAVILLA JR. (EDDIE)
EDWARD HOWARD SR.
EDWARD HOWARD JR. (NED)
EDWARD ALLISON

ARTHUR
ARTHUR DINSMORE
ARTHUR HOWARD (NEPHEW)

FAMILY LINEAGE

WALTER
WALTER DINSMORE
WALTER CONLEY (NEPHEW)
WALTER HOWARD (NEPHEW)
WALTER TRAVILLA (GRAND NEPHEW)

HERBERT
HERBERT CARRINGTON
HERBERT CARRINGTON (NEPHEW)
HERBERT TRAVILLA (NAMESAKE)

HAROLD (HARRY)
HAROLD ALLISON
HARROLD CARRINGTON SR.
HAROLD CARRINGTON JR. (HARRY)
HAROLD TRAVILLA (NAMESAKE H.A.)
HARRY DUNCAN

ARCHIE
ARCHIE CARRINGTON
ARCHIE ROSS (NEPHEW)

SOPHIE
SOPHIE ALLISON CARRINGTON
SOPHIE ROSS (NIECE)

DAISY
DAISY ALLISON
DAISY CARRINGTON (NIECE)

www.ingramcontent.com/pod-product-compliance
Lightning Source LLC
Chambersburg PA
CBHW060006100426
42740CB00010B/1417